JOY TO THE WORLD

JOY TO THE WORLD

Joyce Huggett

eagle

Guildford, Surrey

British Library Cataloguing in Publication Data. A catalogue record for this book is available from the British Library.

Published by Eagle Publishing Ltd, PO Box 530, Guildford, Surrey GU2 4FH.

Scripture quotations are taken from the following translations:
The Holy Bible, New International Version. Copyright © 1973, 1978, 1984 by International Bible Society. Used by permission of Hodder & Stoughton, a division of Hodder Headline.
The Message. Copyright © 1993, 1994, 1995, 1996, 2000. Used by permission of NavPress Publishing Group.
The New English Bible. Copyright © 1961 Cambridge University Press.
The Amplified Bible. Copyright © 1965. Used by permission of Zondervan Bible Publishers.
New Living Translation. Copyright © 1996. Used by permission of Tyndale House Publishers. All rights reserved.
The New Testament, J B Phillips. Translated into modern English by Godfrey Bles (London) 1952, 1956.
New Revised Standard Version. Copyright © 1993. HarperCollins, London.
The New Jerusalem Bible, Standard Edition. Copyright © 1985. Darton, Longman and Todd and Dobleday and Company, Inc.

Typeset by Eagle Publishing
Printed by Clays Ltd, St Ives plc
ISBN No.: 0 86347 373 3

For
'My Anna' (see Meditation 25)
With my love and warm thanks
for decades of care and prayer

Joy to the World

In order that readers might fully appreciate the nature of the meditations featured in this book, Eagle Publishing have produced an accompanying album, available either in CD or cassette tape format, that can be used in conjunction with the text.

The featured tracks are:

Joy to the World
How Great Thou Art
I Cannot Tell
Comfort Ye
Calm Me Lord
Jesus You Are Changing Me
The Father's Song of Love
Brother, Sister, Let Me . . .
Silent Night
Rest in My Love
Mary's Song
O Let the Son of God Enfold You
Jesus is Our Joy
One Thing Have I Asked of the Lord
To Whom Shall We Go?
What Can I Give to the King?
Peace Prayer
Just As I Am

CD: 0 86347495 0
Cassette: 0 86347 494 2

Contents

Acknowledgments

A whole team of people have helped me to bring this book and CD/cassette to birth. My life has been enriched by their support. Here I can mention but a few of them.

First I should like to mention the artists who have generously given me permission to use their visual meditations. Four of these are friends I've known for many years: Sister Theresa Margaret CHN and Gael O'Leary RSM have both worked with me on a number of projects and Joyce Cheverton and Sister Irene CHN whose images have been an inspiration to me for many years.

Two of the artists have become pen-friends even though we've never met: David Chance and Joan Hutson, fellow writer, musician, artist and prayer partner of many years whose support I value more than I can say.

The other two artists are not known to me personally but we have corresponded so much in the bringing to birth of this book that they have become e-mail companions and encouragers to whom I owe a debt of thanks. I feel humbled that they have given me permission to marry their artistic gift with my words and I pray that God will speak as powerfully to my readers through their pictures as he has to me.

Next, I should like to thank the many, many people I contacted as I sought permission to quote the prayers, poetry, prose and songs that appear in the book. Almost all were so kind and courteous and efficient that I felt surrounded by supportive friends rather than strangers who were simply doing a job. In particular, I should like to single out Mo Dingle from SPCK and Ian Corsie of the Northumbria Community for whom nothing seemed to be too much trouble. I am profoundly grateful to them both.

Another person who has worked indefatigably to bring this book into being is Lynne Barratt of Eagle publishing. Thank you, Lynne, for your patience, efficiency, heart-warming encouragement and sheer determination to do all that needed to be done.

Without a publisher, a manuscript will never become a book in a reader's hands. David Wavre has been more than a publisher. By his affirmation and enthusiasm, he has been an encourager and midwife and I'm grateful. It was David who sensed that a CD/cassette would enhance the meditations in the book. I was thrilled by his suggestion and am delighted to be able to share some of my favourite pieces of prayerful music with readers and would-be worshippers. The book does not *need* the CD/cassette. Each meditation stands on its own without music. *With* the multi-media blend of verbal, visual and audio though, the readings and responses are undoubtedly enriched. This makes me profoundly grateful to all who have helped me put this album together – especially my friends Margaret Rizza and Marilyn Baker.

Last, but by no means least, I must mention my husband who read each meditation as it was spewed out by my computer printer. As always, he has enthused and affirmed, supported and encouraged me as well as making invaluable suggestions and constructive criticisms. As ever, he has my heartfelt thanks.

As well as the people mentioned above, I want to thank the unknown number of my readers, supporters and friends who have prayed this book into being. Thank you so much for your letters, your faithfulness, your love and for those all-important prayers.

Joyce Huggett

Introduction

'I hate it! I really *hate* it! I've *always* hated Christmas – ever since I was a little boy! I'll be glad when it's all over.'

That's a snippet of conversation I overheard last year – just three days before Christmas. I was enjoying Christmas shopping in the small town near my home at the time. The agitated, flushed, elderly man who was pouring out his loathing of a time of year that I love was hurrying along the narrow pavement in front of me. The woman who had to rush to keep up with him seemed unperturbed by her husband's tirade. Doubtless she had heard it many times before.

Some fifteen minutes later, while I was choosing pot plants from the pavement outside a florist's shop, a couple came and stood behind me. The woman leaned across me and picked up a beautiful potted 'garden' and eagerly showed it to her partner. He made a comment which I didn't hear but which triggered a violent reaction from the woman. Throwing the pot to the ground she exploded in sheer frustration: 'If you think it's not good enough for your mother, we won't get her *anything*, that's all.' Equally angrily, the man began to argue back as they stormed off into the madding crowd.

A little later, I met my husband in MacDonald's as arranged. While David was queueing for hot chocolate, I thumbed through a copy of the *Daily Mail* that was lying on a shelf. This headline caught my eye:

'One in seven "can't wait for the 27th".'

Intrigued, I read the first sentence: 'Christmas is the dullest time of year for one in seven Britons who say they can't wait for it to end.' The article ended with the conclusion reached by the marketing information service that had questioned 1,000 adults on their view of Christmas: 'While the religious focus of the Christmas period has limited significance, the Christmas meal still clearly provides a strong unifying focus for families.'

The elderly man's expressed loathing of Christmas, the couple's quarrel and the newspaper's claims gnawed at me as I unpacked my Christmas shopping. These attitudes sounded so different from the desires I felt flooding my own heart. They seemed, too, to run contrary to the longings that I had heard expressed just a few days earlier. David and I had been leading an Advent Quiet Day for one hundred Christians who were eager to discover how they could organise their days so that throughout December they could focus on the Christ of Christmas as well as enjoy the celebrations. Together we had explained and explored a variety of ways of fulfilling this dream.

Joy to the World has been written with such people in mind. Many of us approach the beginning of December with eager anticipation. Some make an Advent ring or buy an Advent calendar. Many light an Advent candle and most will decorate a Christmas tree. Early on in December, I like to buy a poinsettia and to take out of their box some of the figures that make up our nativity scene. Instead of putting all the figures out at once, I start by putting the shepherds and the sheep in place. A few days later, the oxen join them. The angel comes next to remind us of the way the Angel Gabriel appeared to Mary. As each animal or person is added to the scene, the sense of anticipation mounts. By Christmas Eve, all the figures are in place except the baby. He comes at midnight after we've attended Holy Communion. By then, we are already experiencing the joy of Christmas.

Each of these gestures can be a prayer. Even so, many of us yearn for more. We ache for time to ponder the mysteries of Advent, Christmas and Epiphany. Advent, with its emphasis on the comings of Christ, Christmas which has the birth of Jesus as its focus and Epiphany with its joyful news that Jesus came, not just for Jews, but for Gentiles too – his love embraces the whole world.

Yes, we long for time to ponder, to wonder, to pray, yet at this stage of our year, time seems even more elusive than usual. So much needs to be squeezed into every hour of every day: shopping for food and presents, writing, receiving and reading Christmas cards and letters, finding the decorations I've already mentioned, putting those decorations in place, preparing to receive family and friends – not to mention the inevitable Carol Services, Christingle Services and celebratory Christmas meals that insist on filling our diaries. As the 'to do' list grows longer by the hour, so our resolve to carve out time to ponder the mysteries that lie at the heart of the Christmas story dwindles or even dies. Yet the desire and the craving claw at us, convincing us that we would find ourselves less stressed if we would heed God's invitation to 'Be still . . .' (Ps 46:10) for a few minutes each day.

The pages of this book are for those who can create or snatch a few focused minutes most days in December. My aim in writing it is to provide readers with a daily Bible passage to read, a reflection to ponder and a response to make to one fragment of the Advent/Christmas/Epiphany story. I picture some readers dipping into the book as they travel to work. I think of mothers of young children thumbing through the pages as they feed the baby or as their children watch *Bob the Builder, Thomas the Tank Engine* or another favourite TV programme or video. And I fondly imagine some who can carve out quality time for reading, pondering and responding in a leisurely way to the wonders of the stories that are so familiar yet somehow so ever-new.

A few of the meditations in the book first appeared in my earlier publication *Approaching Christmas*. Most, however, have either been radically revised or completely re-written. My prayer as this new book goes to print is that, as we marvel again at the wonders of God's love outpoured in the gift to us of his one and only Son, we shall be able to echo the words of the carol from which the title of this book has been borrowed: 'Joy to the World!' This carol, together with many of the other pieces of music that I've mentioned in the book, features on a new CD and cassette created to accompany these meditations. While the book stands on its own and does not need the CD or the cassette, *with* the recorded music, as with the illustrations in the book, our meditations will undoubtedly be enriched. If you have the CD, you might like to start by listening to the theme song *Joy to the World!*

Joyce Huggett
June 2001

Joy to the World

Joy to the world! The Lord is come;
Let earth receive her King,
Let every heart prepare Him room,
And heav'n and nature sing
And heav'n and nature sing
And heav'n and heaven and nature sing!

Joy to the earth! The Saviour reigns;
Let us our songs employ;
While fields and floods, rocks, hills and plains
Repeat the sounding joy,
Repeat the sounding joy,
Repeat, repeat the sounding joy.

He rules the world with truth and grace,
And makes the nations prove,
The glories of His righteousness,
And wonders of His love,
And wonders of His love,
And wonders, wonders of His love.[1]

NOBODY
is an outsider
to this happiness

He's Coming Back!

We shall be with him forever

Chapter One

He's Coming Back

'Well folks! Here's the news you've been waiting for! I'm coming home! I've booked my annual leave and bought my air ticket. I'll be arriving in June and staying for three whole weeks.'

That's the message my brother added to his Christmas card one year. I read the neatly penned words over and over again scarcely daring to believe what I was reading. Eventually, though, the truth trickled into my mind: 'He's coming back! Ray's coming home at last!'

My brother had emigrated to Australia seventeen years earlier. That's why the thought of seeing him again was extra-special. I soon found, however, that I was filled with questions as well as excitement: 'What will the reunion be like?' 'Will we recognise one another?' 'What will we talk about?' 'What will we do?'

My brother came. We *did* recognise each other. When we met, at first we said nothing. Instead, we each opened our arms for the other and simply held each other in a long, lingering, loving embrace. Eventually, though, we found that we couldn't cram into three weeks all that we wanted to say to sum up seventeen years apart and to recall countless childhood memories.

God's letter from home, as St Augustine called the Bible, carries an even more amazing message: *Jesus is coming back. When he comes, he will take us to be with himself for ever:*

*One word of command, one shout from the archangel, one
blast from the trumpet of God and the Lord himself will
come down from Heaven! Those who have died in Christ
will be the first to rise, and then we who are still living will
be swept up with them into the clouds to meet the Lord in
the air. And after that we shall be with him for ever. So by
all means use this message to encourage one another.*

(1 Thes 4:16–18 JBP)

'The Lord himself will come down from Heaven' (v 16).
That's the theme for this first week of meditations. The word
'come' is the buzz-word for Advent. 'Come' is a word full of
longing and anticipation and preparation. As Carlo Carretto
puts it: 'Come, Lord Jesus' (Rev 22:20) is a summing up of all
the impassioned prayers uttered after the departure of Christ.[1]
The word 'Come' occurs in Advent carol after Advent carol:

Lo! He comes, with clouds descending,
Once for favoured sinners slain;
Thousand, thousand saints attending
Swell the triumph of His train;
Hallelujah!
Christ appears on earth to reign.
(John Cennick, Charles Wesley and Martin Madan)

A Response

How do you imagine you will act and react when Jesus returns?

Write a prayer of your own, telling Jesus how you feel about his
impending return.

If you have the *Joy to the World* CD, listen to the hymn *How
Great Thou Art*. Join in if it helps you to worship.

Use one or more of the following three prayers:

O Lord, give us yourself above all things.
It is in your coming alone that we are enriched.
It is in your coming that your true gifts come.
Come, Lord, that we may share the gifts of your Presence.
Come, Lord, with healing of the past,
Come and calm our memories,
Come with joy for the present,
Come and give life to our existence,
Come with hope for the future,
Come and give a sense of eternity.
Come with strength for our will,
Come with power for our thoughts,
Come with love for our heart,
Come and give affection to our being.
Come, Lord, give yourself above all things,
And help us to give ourselves to you.[2]

* * *

Come, Lord God, change us and we shall be changed.
Come, increase our awareness of your presence.
Come, strengthen our love for you.
Come, fill our hearts with holiness.
Come, awaken us to be ready and watchful for your coming.
Come, Lord God, change us and we shall be changed;
through him who lives and reigns with you and the Holy Spirit,
one God, now and for ever. Amen[3]

Can it be true, Jesus?
You are returning
to take me home with you?
Sometimes the thought thrills me.
I long to be with you forever.
Sometimes the thought fills me with dread:
I'm not ready for you,
Life here is so good
I don't want you to return just yet.
Forgive my doubting
Melt my coldness
Fill me with fresh awe
as I ponder the mysteries
surrounding your promised return.
Then I shall want to change
and be changed.
Then I shall be ready to drop everything to
come to you
to greet you with heartfelt thanks
and everlasting joy
no matter when you come.[4]

Chapter Two

How Will He Come?

One evening, while I was on holiday on the island of Cyprus, I sat on the shore of a salt lake marvelling at the wonder of the sunset. The tranquil lake reflected the beauty of the gold ball suspended in the sky. As I watched, though, a black line seemed to divide the sun into two parts. This apparent fissure deepened as the now-red ball was swallowed up by the darkening mountain range.

An hour later, while I lay relaxing in a warm bath and reliving the wonder of that sunset, my reveries were rudely interrupted by the din of furniture being scraped to and fro on the tiled floor of the flat above. To my horror, the bath in which I sat then began to shudder. 'What's happening?' I yelled to my husband. 'It's an earthquake!' he shouted against the noise. 'You'd better get some clothes on quick!'

Earlier that day, David and I had been discussing the Scripture Union notes that I was currently writing. My subject was 'The Second Coming of Christ' so, as I grabbed some clothes and hastily pulled them on, certain prophecies buzzed around my brain – like this one:

'Sun will fade out,
      moon cloud over,
Stars fall out of the sky,
      Cosmic powers tremble.'

'Then, the Arrival of the Son of Man! It will fill the skies –
no one will miss it. Unready people all over the world,
outsiders to the splendour and power, will raise a huge
lament as they watch the Son of Man blazing out of heaven.
At that same moment, he'll dispatch his angels with a
trumpet-blast summons, pulling in God's chosen from the
four winds, from pole to pole.'

(Mt 24:29–31 The Message)

Outside the apartment block, I saw, not the wonders Jesus
describes, but a group of silent, ashen-faced residents. Many
were Lebanese women with frightened children clinging to
their long skirts. Having fled the trauma of the then war-torn
Beirut, they were clearly shocked to be plunged so unexpectedly
into terror of a different kind. Together we watched – and
waited a long, agonising wait. Nothing happened. The building
did not collapse. The rumblings ceased. Gradually the crowd
dispersed, most people returning, somewhat fearfully, to their
apartment. Dazed, David and I wandered to a nearby taverna.
We ate by candlelight because, thanks to the earthquake, there
was no electricity. For the second time that day, we talked
about the second coming of Jesus. This time our discussion was
more sober. It was as though we had had a foretaste that had
made a deep and double impact on us both. On the one hand
we felt full of awe. On the other hand, our hearts ached for
those living nearby who had never yet heard the name of Jesus.
Next day, I resumed my writing on the second coming of
Christ with a great deal more feeling than the day before!

A Response

In his book *The Jesus Hope*, Stephen Travis writes:

> The hope of Christ's return is not a dogma to tickle our
> brains, but a fact to change our lives. Whenever the
> Bible speaks about Christ's second coming its purpose is
> always to challenge us to action . . . We are living
> 'between the times' – between the time when Jesus
> introduced God's new era and the time when he will
> return to establish God's kingdom in its final form.
> Waiting for that momentous event is not a matter of
> sitting in our back gardens with our telescopes scanning
> the horizon. It is not a matter of killing time like waiting
> for a late train. It is a time for action, a time for
> distinctive Christian living.[1]

If you knew for certain that Jesus was to return in one week's
time, what might you do to prepare for his coming?
Write a prayer telling Jesus how you would prepare for his
return.

* * *

Metropolitan Anthony Bloom once wrote:

> We must learn to behave in the presence of the invisible
> Lord as we would in the presence of the Lord made
> visible to us. This implies primarily an attitude of mind
> and then its reflection upon the body. If Christ was here,
> before us, and we stood completely transparent to his
> gaze, in mind as well as in body, we would feel reverence,
> the fear of God, adoration or else perhaps terror but we
> should not be so easy in our behaviour as we are.[2]

Re-read that claim then ask yourself, 'If Jesus stood beside or in front of me now, how might I feel? What changes might take place in my behaviour patterns?'

* * *

Read the words of the hymn *I Cannot Tell* . . . as slowly as possible until a word or a phrase or a pen-picture draws you to itself. Then stop and sit with your word or picture before talking to God about the impact it has made on you. If you have the *Joy to the World* CD, listen to the hymn *I Cannot Tell* today.

A Prayer

May I anticipate your Second Coming
With joy, Jesus.
And when you do appear,
May you find me ready:
With face upturned to greet you,
Arms opened wide to welcome you,
A song of praise on my lips to worship you,
A heart aflame with love for you
Expressing itself
in the care of your poor.[3]

I cannot tell . . .

I cannot tell how He will win the nations,
how He will claim His earthly heritage,
how satisfy the needs and aspirations
of East and West, of sinner and of sage,
but this I know, all flesh shall see His glory
and He shall reap the harvest He has sown,
and some glad day His sun shall shine
in splendour
when He, the Saviour, Saviour of the
world is known.

I cannot tell how all the lands shall worship,
when, at His bidding, every storm is stilled,
or who can say how great the jubilation
when ev'ry heart with perfect love is filled.
But this I know, the skies will thrill with rapture
and myriad, myriad human voices sing
and earth to heaven, and heaven to
earth will answer:
at last the Saviour, Saviour of the world, is King![4]

Chapter Three

When Will He Come?

For centuries, Christians have tried to predict the precise date on which Jesus will return. As the year 1000 approached, the level of excitement rose. Surely the Lord would choose to return in this year? He did not come. In the twelfth century, a certain monk estimated that the world would end between 1200 and 1260. It did not. In more recent times, Jehovah's Witnesses speculated that the world as we know it would cease to exist in 1975. It did not. Neither had the present age closed in 1874, 1914, or 1915 as had been anticipated. Most recently of all, a number of Christians insisted that Jesus would return as the year 2000 dawned. Believing that he would return in Israel, to the alarm of the authorities in that country, fanatics and others flocked to that land where Jesus lived when he came to us as man. He did not come.

When will we learn, I wonder, that to spend hours calculating the date of the second coming is not only a waste of time, it is to miss the point of the clear teaching of Jesus himself. Even he claimed complete ignorance of the date of his return:

Jesus said:

'The exact day and hour? No one knows that, not even heaven's angels, not even the Son. Only the Father knows. 'The Arrival of the Son of Man will take place in times like

Noah's. Before the great flood everyone was carrying on as usual, having a good time right up to the day Noah boarded the ark. They knew nothing – until the flood hit and swept everything away.

'The Son of Man's Arrival will be like that: Two men will be working in the field – one will be taken, one left behind; two women will be grinding at the mill – one will be taken, one left behind. So stay awake, alert. You have no idea what day your Master will show up. But you do know this: You know that if the homeowner had known what time of night the burglar would arrive, he would have been there with his dogs to prevent the break-in. Be vigilant just like that. You have no idea when the Son of Man is going to show up.'

(Mt 24:36–44 The Message)

The readiness Jesus refers to is *heart-readiness* – the kind of heart-change that, quoting Isaiah 40, John the Baptist describes so colourfully:

'Prepare God's arrival!
Make the road smooth and straight!
Every ditch will be filled in,
Every bump smoothed out,
The detours straightened out,
All the ruts paved over.
Everyone will be there to see
The parade of God's salvation.'

(Lk 3:4b–6 The Message)

The picture John paints is a powerful one – of a road so riddled with ruts, rocks and detours that journeys become treacherous – like the detours and dead-ends in today's picture. Look carefully at that picture. Compare and contrast the smooth, straight path on which the couple make their way to the Christ-child with the tortuous, futile paths that criss-cross the picture or with the weapons and wealth that you can see. Do the weapons of war, the sea creatures, the fishing boats or the frenzy of paths speak to you of any part of your own life? Compare these with the serene, focused figures facing Jesus. If you could put yourself in the picture, where would you be?

The picture reminds us that preparing the way for the King demands drastic action – the removal of the rocks for one thing and the filling up and smoothing over of the ruts for another. When his followers asked him *how* they were to make these changes in preparation for the Messiah's coming, John the Baptist urged them to *repent*:

> *'Repent, for the kingdom of heaven is near.'*
>
> (Mt 3:2)

To repent starts by recognising and admitting where we have been grieving God. It continues by plucking up the courage to come into God's presence even though we are as soiled and bedraggled spiritually as the prodigal son was when he returned to his father. It then involves the humility to receive God's outpoured love and forgiveness. Repentance is completed by finishing the U-turn: that is, turning our back on the behaviour and belongings that have hurt the God who loves us and, with an act of the will, turning our faces *towards* this God once more. In this way we prepare the way for God to come to us and for us to make our return to him.

A Response

Ask the Holy Spirit to show you where rocks and ruts have ruined the road that links you with God. Listen to his voice as he highlights and names the rocks that need to be removed and the ruts that need to be filled in. Repent in the way that I have just described even though this may take weeks rather than hours.

A road riddled with detours

Now spend time receiving the forgiveness and love that God is offering to you.

*   *   *

Read the following message that God gave through Isaiah, putting your own name in the place where you see the **** and changing 'her sin' to 'his sin' if you are a man!

> *'Comfort, oh comfort my people . . .*
> *Speak softly and tenderly to ****
> *make it very clear . . .*
> *that her sin is taken care of – forgiven! . . .*
> *and now it's over and done with.'*
>
> (Is 40:1 The Message)

Read those words over and over again until the message has sunk deep into your heart. You are forgiven. When you are ready, ask God to give you the grace to live differently. Then, if you can, pray this prayer:

*Lord, turn my **whole being** to your praise and glory.*

If you have the *Joy to the World* CD, listen to the *Comfort ye . . .* track from *Handel's Messiah* as you continue to let God's forgiveness seep into your soul.

A Prayer

O Lord
My years grow long
And my time short
Let me make haste with my repentance
And bow both my head and heart
Let me not stay one day from amendment
Lest I stay too long
Let me cease without delay
To love my own mischief
And to abandon, without a backward look
The unfruitful works of darkness.
Lord, grant me new watchfulness
To lay hold upon opportunity for good
Make me at last put on the whole armour of light
Rank me among those who work for their Lord
Loins girded, lamps burning
Till the night shall pass
And the true light shine
Let me sing the new song
Following the lamb wherever he goes
Loving wherever he loves
Doing whatever he bids
Until the perfect day
The day of the true Advent
When the light comes into the world
For ever and ever.[1]

Chapter Four

No More Pain

In the past few days, we have focused on the fact of Jesus' return: *He's coming back*. We have focused, too, on the way in which he will return and the continued uncertainty about the date of his return. For the next three days, we shift the emphasis to another question that people often ask: *What will his coming be like?* To apply our minds and hearts to this question, we turn to the book of Revelation where we hear the wonderful news that when Jesus returns there will be no more pain.

Imagine how Jesus' close friend, John, must have felt when he received this good news. He was on the beautiful Greek island of Patmos but his circumstances were far from idyllic. He was in exile and, if tradition is to be believed, his living accommodation was a small, dark cave not far from the highest point on the island. There, in that dingy cave, John was praying 'in the Spirit' one Sabbath day. As he prayed, he was given the immense privilege of sensing and seeing in picture form what life will be like when Jesus returns. He also received specific instructions from God to record the vision, and one of the things that intrigues pilgrims to Patmos is to see that, in the

cave, there is a 'desk' made of stone where some believe John
stood to capture on papyrus what he had seen:

> *I saw a new heaven and a new earth, for the old heaven and
> the old earth had disappeared. And the sea was also gone.
> And I saw the holy city, the new Jerusalem, coming down
> from God out of heaven like a beautiful bride prepared for
> her husband.*
>
> *I heard a loud shout from the throne, saying, 'Look, the
> home of God is now among his people! God himself will be
> with them, their God. He will remove all of their sorrows,
> and there will be no more death or sorrow or crying or pain.
> For the old world and its evils are gone forever.'*
>
> (Rev 21:1–4 NLT)

A nine-year-old Nigerian boy was butchered to death in
London a week before I sat down to write this reflection. Today
would have been his tenth birthday and television cameras captured some of the moving sentiments that were expressed in the
Birthday Memorial Service that was held in the packed church
where he worshipped three times each week. The memories
that fill my mind as I write are of the courageous, faith-filled
but grief-stricken family.

The weekend before this service was held, my own little
granddaughter was whisked into hospital where she found
herself in a ward full of sick babies and where she was given
oxygen to help her breathing. I remember the pain that stabbed
me when I heard that the little girl I love was so unwell. I remember, too, the sadness that filled me when a friend of mine
died on Christmas Eve and when, a few days later, I heard that
a former secretary of mine had also died.

Sadness and pain, goodbyes and grief are familiar to us all.
No wonder today's Advent reading is a favourite. It reminds us
that, when Jesus returns, life will no longer be a mixture of joy
and pain, disappointments and dreams, frustrations and

friendships, loneliness and love. Tears will no longer be our meat day and night, as the psalmist so colourfully describes life here on earth. Instead, there will be no more crying and sighing, loss and sorrow. The thought of a time and place where tears and loss and sorrow and sighing cease for ever seems almost too good to be true yet this was the assurance that John was given high up on that island hill.

A Response

Write a prayer telling God how you feel about the news that the day is coming when pain will become a thing of the past. Then, if you have the *Joy to the World* CD listen to the soothing song called *Calm Me Lord*.

A Prayer

It is possible even now to have a foretaste of peace being poured into pain. The following prayer paves the way for such an experience:

Jesus,
your care for me –
passionate
compassionate
relentlessly tender
tried
true –
breathes balm into my battered soul
pours peace into my grieving heart
speaks certainty into my agitated spirit
causes hope to rise like a phoenix
from the ashes of my pain.

Lord, I lay before you my life
All my yesterdays,
My todays and tomorrows.
I praise and thank you for your presence
in my life.
I lift up in gratitude all the goodness and
all the joy.
I now offer you all my hurts, my bruises,
my rejection,
I offer you all those things of which
I am ashamed
What I have said, and done, and thought,
All that has brought hurt to you and to others.
Lord pour your cleansing streams of living water
all over me.
Make the parched deserts of my being
spring to life
Refresh me, Renew me.
Lord breathe on me afresh now
And I will receive your life.
Lord reach out and touch me and I will receive
your healing.[1]

Chapter Five

No More Striving

Author Trina Paulus tells the story of a caterpillar whose name was *Yellow*. She used to dream of becoming a butterfly but doubted that this liberating phenomenon could ever happen to her:

> *'How can I believe there's a butterfly inside me when all I can see is a fuzzy worm?'*

One day, Yellow met a fellow caterpillar which encouraged her to believe that she could be transformed. She decided to take the risk: to lose the life she knew, the caterpillar state, and to weave around herself the cocoon from which she would emerge as a butterfly. Her friends waited with bated breath.

Their patience was rewarded. Rising from the chrysalis, before their very eyes, was a brilliant, yellow, winged creature; it was the same **Yellow** they had always known and yet so very different. She looked splendid as she soared into the sky, circled round and gloried in the air she had now inherited. Her freedom was intoxicating.

The apostle Paul, writing to the Christians in Rome, reminds us that, while this life lasts, we, too, are rather like caterpillars, 'groaning inwardly while we wait for God to . . . set our whole body free' (Rom 8:22 NEB). Paul also encourages us to believe that, when Jesus returns, we shall no longer need to strive to be like him; the transformation will be instant and complete:

> *Let me tell you a wonderful secret God has revealed to us. Not all of us will die, but we will all be transformed. It will happen in a moment, in the blinking of an eye, when the last trumpet is blown. For when the trumpet sounds, the Christians who have died will be raised with transformed bodies. And then we who are living will be transformed so that we will never die. For our perishable earthly bodies must be transformed into heavenly bodies that will never die.*
>
> *When this happens – when our perishable earthly bodies have been transformed into heavenly bodies that will never die – then at last the Scriptures will come true:*
>
> > *'Death is swallowed up in victory.*
> > *O death, where is your victory?*
> > *O death, where is your sting?'*
>
> *. . . How we thank God, who gives us victory over sin and death through Jesus Christ our Lord!*
>
> > (1 Cor 15:51–57 NLT)

In other words, when Jesus returns, we shall be free at last: free from death, free from struggling and striving, free to be the person God created us to be.

A Response

If you have a CD or tape of Handel's *Messiah*, listen to the track: 'The Trumpet Shall Sound'. Let the good news thrill you: 'We shall be changed.'

* * *

Write a prayer in which you spread before God those areas of your life that need a transforming touch. Now pause to be aware that God loves you *now* – before you have changed. Drink in that love. More than anything else in the world this will motivate you to *want* to change and be changed. Thank God that, because of his grace, he *is* changing you. None of us can change on our own! Then, if you have the *Joy to the World* CD, listen to Marilyn Baker's reassuring prayer-song: *Jesus, You are changing me*. Let it be your personal prayer for today.

Jesus, You are changing me
By your Spirit, you're making me like You.
Jesus, you're transforming me
That your loveliness may be seen in all I do.
You are the potter and I am the clay,
Make me to be willing, to let you have your way,
Jesus, You are changing me
'Till I let you reign supreme within my heart.[1]

Chapter Six

The End of Evil

One of the most beautiful pen-pictures in the Bible appears in Genesis 1:31. The world with all its wonders has been created and we find Creator God enjoying everything that he has made. 'He saw it was excellent in every way' (Gen 1:31 NLT). Conversely, one of the most tragic pen-pictures painted in the Bible appears just five chapters later:

> *Now the LORD observed the extent of the people's wickedness, and he saw that all their thoughts were consistently and totally evil. So the LORD was sorry he had ever made them. It broke his heart.*
>
> (Gen 6:5 NLT)

We, too, can break God's heart – by turning our backs on his love and caving in to temptation's allure. That is why Peter, James and Paul issue these spiritual health warnings:

> *Be careful! Watch out for attacks from the Devil, your great enemy . . . Take a firm stand against him . . .*
>
> (1 Pet 5:8–9 NLT)

> *Yell a loud **no** to the Devil and watch him scamper. Say a quiet yes to God and he'll be there in no time.*
>
> (Jas 4:7,8 The Message)

*Stand **against** the Devil's evil tricks . . . resist the
enemy's attacks.*

(Eph 6:11,13 GNB)

Resisting temptation, yelling 'no' to the tempter and
whispering 'yes' to God is rarely easy. So often Satan's
suggestions seem so sensible, so plausible, so attractive, so right.
Yet they come tailor-made to sidetrack us: away from God
towards self-destruction because they come from the mind of
one who is evil through and through. As Jim Packer puts it, the
Bible encourages us to believe in 'a Satan and a host of Satanic
myrmidons, who are of quite unimaginable badness – more
cruel, more malicious, more proud, more scornful, more
perverted, more destructive, more disgusting, more filthy, more
despicable, than anything our minds can conceive'.[1]

He not only implants evil thoughts into our minds and
dresses temptation up to make it look attractive, he inflicts
illness and diseases on people, oppresses them, holds them in
spiritual bondage, performs counterfeit miracles, beguiles them
into believing that his suggestions and plans are best. When
Jesus returns, all this will change. As John reminds us, this was
one reason why he came: 'The reason the Son of God appeared
was to destroy the devil's work' (1 Jn 3:8).

In his vision on the island of Patmos, God revealed to John
the dramatic way in which this would take place:

*I saw an Angel descending out of Heaven. He carried the key
to the Abyss and a chain – a huge chain. He grabbed the
Dragon, that old Snake – the very Devil, Satan himself! –
chained him up for a thousand years, dumped him into the
Abyss, slammed it shut and sealed it tight. No more trouble
out of him, deceiving the nations – until the thousand years
are up. After that he has to be let loose briefly . . .*

*When the thousand years are up, Satan will be let loose
from his cell, and will launch again his old work of deceiving*

the nations, searching out victims in every nook and cranny of earth . . . He'll talk them into going to war and will gather a huge army, millions strong. They'll stream across the earth, surround and lay siege to the camp of God's holy people, the Beloved City. They'll no sooner get there than fire will pour out of Heaven and burn them up. The Devil who deceived them will be hurled into Lake Fire and Brimstone, joining the Beast and False Prophet, the three in torment around the clock for ages without end.

(Rev 20:1–3; 7–10 The Message)

This terrifying and gruesome picture resolves into a description of the glory and joy of the new Jerusalem:

> *I heard a voice thunder from the Throne: 'Look! Look! God has moved into the neighbourhood, making his home with men and women! They're his people, he's their God. He'll wipe every tear from their eyes. Death is gone for good – tears gone, crying gone, pain gone . . . I'm making everything new.'*

(Rev 21:3–5 The Message)

A Response

Praise the Name of Jesus by echoing these words of Charles Wesley:

> Jesus! The name high over all,
> In hell, or earth, or sky;
> Angels and men before it fall,
> And devils fear and fly.
>
> Jesus the prisoner's fetters breaks
> And bruises Satan's head;
> Power into strengthless souls it speaks,
> And life into the dead.
>
> Happy, if with my latest breath
> I might but gasp His name;
> Preach Him to all, and cry in death;
> Behold, behold the Lamb!

Thank Jesus that, just as he was committed to Peter and prayed specifically for him that he should not be beguiled by Satan, so he prays for us:

> *'Simon, Simon, do you know that Satan has asked to have you all to sift you like wheat? – but I have prayed for you that you may not lose your faith. Yes, when you have turned back to me, you must strengthen these brothers of yours.'*
> (Lk 22:31 JBP)

Read that verse again putting your own name at the beginning instead of 'Simon'.

Try to picture Jesus praying *for you*. How does it feel to be assured that he is praying for you today and always?

* * *

Recall how Jesus was assaulted by Satan while he was on retreat in the desert (Matt 4:1 ff). Ask God for the grace to send Satan packing in the authoritative way that Jesus did with the command: 'Get behind me, Satan.'

Read and pray the hymn on the next page:

Breathe on me breath of God,
Fill me with life anew,
That I may love what Thou dost love
And do what Thou woulds't do.

Breathe on me, Breath of God,
Until my heart is pure,
Until with Thee I will one will,
To do and to endure.

Breathe on me, Breath of God,
Till I am wholly Thine,
Until this earthly part of me
Glows with Thy fire divine.

Breathe on me, Breath of God,
So shall I never die,
But live with Thee the perfect life
Of Thine eternity.[2]

Chapter Seven

For Ever With The Lord

At the end of John Bunyan's book *Pilgrim's Progress*, the hero of the story, Christian, comes at last to the river over which he must cross before he enters the Holy City: the New Jerusalem: Heaven. Ministering spirits come to encourage him as he embarks on the last lap of the journey. They describe to him what life will be like when he reaches the other side:

'There,' said they, 'is the Mount Sion, the heavenly Jerusalem, the innumerable company of angels, and the spirits of just men made perfect; you are going now . . . to the Paradise of God . . . and when you come there you shall have white robes given you, and your walk and talk shall be every day with the King, even all the days of eternity. There you shall not see again such things as you saw when you were in the lower region upon the earth: sorrow, sickness, affliction and death, for the former things are passed away . . .

Then I heard in my dream, that all the bells in the City rang again for joy; and that it was said unto them, 'Enter into the favour of your Lord'. I also heard the men themselves, that they sang with a loud voice, saying, 'Blessing, honour, glory and power be to him that sitteth upon the throne, and to the Lamb for ever and ever.'[1]

The apostle John gives us another glimpse of the joy that

will be ours when Jesus comes to claim us for himself:

*I looked again. I saw a huge crowd, too huge to count.
Everyone was there – all nations and tribes, all races and
languages. And they were standing, dressed in white robes
and waving palm branches, standing before the Throne and
the Lamb and heartily singing:*

> *'Salvation to our God on his Throne!
> Salvation to the Lamb!'*

*All who were standing around the Throne – Angels, Elders,
Animals – fell on their faces before the Throne and
worshipped God, singing:*

> *'Oh, Yes!
> The blessing and glory and wisdom and thanks-*
giving,
> *The honor and power and strength,
> To our God forever and ever and ever! . . .*

> *Then I heard the sound of massed choirs, the sound of
> a mighty cataract, the sound of strong thunder:*

> *'Hallejujah!*

*The Master reigns,
     our God, the Sovereign-Strong!
Let us celebrate, let us rejoice,
     let us give him the glory!
The Marriage of the Lamb has come;
     his Wife has made herself ready.
She was given a bridal gown
     of bright and shining linen.
The linen is the righteousness of the saints.'*

The river over which he must cross

The Angel said to me, 'Write this: "Blessed are those invited to the Wedding Supper of the Lamb." ' He added, 'These are the true words of God!'

(Rev 7:9; 11–12; 19:6–9 The Message)

A Response

Write a prayer telling God how you feel about the part of John's vision that we are focussing on today. Or respond to these readings with pastels or paints – expressing your feelings in colour.

If you have the *Joy to the World* CD listen to the hymn *How Great Thou Art*, listening especially to the last verse.

A Prayer

Eternal Light, shine into our hearts,
Eternal Goodness, deliver us from evil,
Eternal Power, be our support,
Eternal Wisdom, scatter the darkness
of our ignorance,
Eternal Pity, have mercy upon us;
That with all our heart and mind and
soul and strength
We may seek thy face and be brought by thine
infinite mercy
To thy holy presence;
Through Jesus Christ our Lord.
Amen[2]

He's Here

Chapter Eight

In The Ordinary

One of my heroes of the faith is Brother Lawrence, the monastery cook who insisted that he experienced God's closeness in the monastery kitchen just as keenly as he did in the monastery chapel. I can well understand why people flocked to this seventeenth-century monk to learn the art of practising the presence of God – that is, tuning into the presence and the love of God wherever we are, whatever we are doing.

Brother Lawrence insisted that, since God is everywhere, we can hear him and sense him and talk to him and experience his closeness at any time of day or night. I was turning these claims over in my mind just after Christmas one year as I set out for a brisk afternoon walk. There was time only to explore the maze of streets that surrounds the retreat centre where I was staying. I returned from that walk glowing inside and out: my cheeks were glowing from the crispness and freshness of the air and my heart was glowing and excited from the way God had met me through ordinary, Christmassy things almost every step of the way.

The first thing that stopped me in my tracks was a magnificent holly bush in a garden only yards from where I was staying. Not only was it tall and stately but every branch seemed to be so laden with berries that I could understand why the holly tree is sometimes likened to the burning bush. My mind went, too, to other legends that surround this bush that comes into its own at this time of year. Some Christians, for example, liken the holly that looks so resplendent in the winter sunshine, to Mary who seemed aglow with the Spirit as she praised God in the words of the Magnificat. Others liken scarlet holly berries to the drops of blood that trickled down the face of Jesus as the crown of thorns broke his flesh. With these thoughts swirling round my mind, I stopped and gawked at that magnificent bush for several minutes before journeying on.

The front door of almost every home in this neighbour-hood, it seemed, boasted an evergreen wreath. Without wanting to be rude, again, at times, I just had to stop and stare as I recalled the symbolism that has been attached to such celebrations of Christmas. For the ancient Romans, for example, evergreens became emblems of peace and joy and victory. The early Christians adapted this symbol by placing wreaths of holly and ivy, pine and fir in their windows to indicate that Christ had entered their home. Since evergreens are always green and always alive this symbolism was particularly powerful, suggesting that when Jesus, the ever-living, never-changing One enters our home, he comes to stay.

As well as an evergreen wreath, almost every home seemed to have acquired a Christmas tree and as the sun began to set, so the lights on the trees were switched on: some shone steadily, others flashed on and off, on and off. The fairy-tale beauty of the effect reminded me of the way Christmas trees became popular in Europe. One Christmas Eve, so the story goes, Martin Luther wandered outside and gazed with awe and wonder at the brilliance and beauty of the star-lit sky. His mind flew back in time to the night of the Saviour's birth and over in space to Bethlehem whose skies became the platform for the pageant of the angels on this night. Longing to share with his wife and children the awe and wonder that had filled him, on his way home he cut from the forest an evergreen tree that still glistened with snow. At home, he decorated the tree with candles to remind him and his family of the glory that flooded heaven and earth on the night Jesus was born.

With this story in my mind, the word 'glory' was uppermost in my thoughts when I returned to the Convent. I made my way to the chapel to thank God for his goodness and there, in the hushed stillness, a flower arrangement that had been put in place while I was walking took my breath away. Its position, its shape and its scarlet and lemon carnations that toned so beautifully with the nearby picture of Mary and her baby shrieked glory so powerfully that all I could do was to kneel in wonder, love and praise. As I knelt, the scent of the freesias that had been placed by the crib seemed like incense adding to the wonder of the moment.

The Christmas story revolves around and revels in one example after another of God's glory bursting into the humdrum of the ordinary. Take the second chapter of Luke's Gospel, for example. There we see ordinary shepherds watching ordinary sheep in an ordinary field on the outskirts of an ordinary town when:

> *Suddenly, God's angel stood among them and God's glory blazed around them. They were terrified. The angel said, 'Don't be afraid. I'm here to announce a great and joyful event that is meant for everybody, worldwide: A Saviour has just been born in David's town, a Saviour who is Messiah and Master.'*
>
> (Lk 2:8–11 The Message)

As though the contrast between the humdrum of the nightly duty and the glory of the vast host of worshipping angels was not enough, the angel continued: 'This is how you will recognize him: You will find a baby lying in a manger, wrapped snugly in strips of cloth!' (Lk 2:12 NLT).

The Messiah in a manger wrapped in swaddling clothes! God sanctifying the ordinary!

A Response

Professor Kenneth Bailey claims that the shepherds plucked up courage to visit the new-born baby Messiah because he had been born in a home just like theirs; because he had been wrapped in pieces of cloth just like peasant babies were. Because they plucked up courage to obey the message of the angels, they encountered God's glory in extraordinary circumstances:

Our God contracted to a span
Incomprehensibly made man.[1]

Spend some time today simply adoring the Christ-child. Then, write a prayer telling God how you feel about his willingness to permeate our ordinariness.

Brother Lawrence claimed that 'God is everywhere, in all places and there is no spot where we cannot draw near to Him and hear Him speaking in our heart: with a little love, just a very little, we shall not find it hard.'[2]

Similarly, David Adam observes how this philosophy lay at the heart of Celtic spirituality:

> There was for them a Divine Immanence that helped them to transcend much that was dull routine and hard labour. They talked naturally to God as a man or woman talks to a friend. They rejoiced in a closeness and were sure of His help. Through Him, a glory was theirs, a glory that made the world quite a different place, for they were never alone. Whether they needed guidance, a helping hand or a companion, they could turn to the Friend and say 'God'.[3]

Look for hints of God's glory today. When his glory bursts into the ordinariness, pause for a moment if you can and *marvel* and *enjoy* it to the full. If you have time, write a simple prayer-poem that captures the moment – like this:

Raindrops

Raindrops dangling
    like bright baubles
        on the fronds of the bottle-brush tree.
Enjoy them.[4]

Prayer

Lord, may we love
    And respect
        All your creation,
All the earth
        And every grain of sand in it.
May we love every leaf,
    And every ray of light.[5]

Joy

As the hand is made for holding
And the eye for seeing,
You have fashioned me, O Lord,
For joy.
Share with me the vision:

To
find
that joy
everywhere:
In the holly
berry's beauty,
In the owl's melody,
In the flame of a candle,
In a person of compassion,
In the shining eyes of a child,
In the love of friends and family,
In Christmas lights
And star-lit sky
And most of all
In Jesus.[6]

Chapter Nine

In People

God comes to us in the ordinary; God also comes to us in people. A small boy once underlined this for his father while they were on a father–son holiday together. They settled happily into their hotel and, after the boy had had his supper, the father read him a story and put him to bed. As his father prepared to go downstairs for *his* meal, however, the child began to cry. When his father asked him the reason for the tears, his son clung to him: 'I don't want you to leave me. I'm scared.'

'There's no need to be frightened,' his father consoled him. 'I'll leave the light on and anyway, God is here with you.'

'Yes!' replied the boy. 'But just for tonight, I'd like my God with skin on!'

I once attended a conference at a time in my life when I felt very fragile for a whole variety of reasons. No one at the conference knew me well enough to suspect that behind the smile with which I greeted them lay an aching heart. Yet through the care and prayer and love that they lavished on me, God held me and healed the pain that had lain hidden and festering for many years. Each member of that conference became for me 'God with skin on' in a way I shall never forget.

At this time of year, most of us receive messages of love from relatives, friends and acquaintances – through phone-calls and Christmas cards, e-mails and gifts. Author Macrina Wieder-kehr persuades us not just to rip open the envelopes of a

Christmas card or letter, quickly cast an eye over its message and add it to the pile.

'Always serve letters with a cup of tea and a footstool,' she suggests. 'Celebrate "the reading" slowly. It is irreverent to read a letter fast.'[1]

She goes on to reveal how she treasures her letters 'like early morning sunrises'.[2] She sees the rays between the lines, hears the dreams and the yearnings, the gratitude and the delight. Such savouring of letters and cards and e-mails reaps a rich reward. God speaks to us, touches us, loves us through the ordinariness of the mail-bag or Internet. God touches us, not once, but many times as we return to the written messages over and over again.

In her powerful composition, *The Father's Song of Love*, Marilyn Baker reminds us that God is always attempting to persuade us that we are intimately and uniquely loved. She has God saying to *us*:

All I want to do is to bless you,
All I want to do is pour out my love
To show you how dear you are to me,
*   For me there is no other,*
To me, you are the pearl of great price.[3]

Marilyn's message finds its roots in John's pastoral letter but John goes further. He reminds us that in-poured love has to find an outlet:

This is how God showed his love for us: God sent his only Son into the world so we might live through him. This is the kind of love we are talking about – not that we once upon a time loved God, but that he loved us and sent his Son as a sacrifice to clear away our sins and the damage they've done to our relationship with God.

My dear, dear friends, if God loved us like this, we certainly ought to love each other. No one has seen God, ever. But if we love one another, God dwells deeply within us, and his love becomes complete in us – perfect love!

This is how we know we're living steadily and deeply in him, and he in us: He's given us life from his life, from his very own Spirit . . . We know it so well, we've embraced it heart and soul, this love that comes from God.

(1 Jn 4:9–13, 16 The Message)

A Resolve

Since Christmas cards usually arrive at a time when we feel least like reading them, instead of throwing them away as soon as you take them down, resolve to re-read them in the New Year – enjoying to the full their messages of love. Thank God that the love of each of your friends is but a pale reflection of the divine love.

A Response

As I look around my study, I see photographs of each member of my family, one of my closest friend, one of my Spiritual Mentor, two of places where I go away to seek stillness and time alone with God. Each reminds me of the richness of God's love. In my study, too, I see colourful bookmarks woven for me by a friend in Lebanon, a postcard from someone here in England, a crocheted star made by a refugee overseas and sent to me by one of my many missionary friends. Each of these photographs and gifts remind me that God comes to me through those who love me.

Look around *your* home at your own photographs and treasures. Recall how and when they came to you and thank God that he chooses to convey his love to you through people.

If you have the *Joy to the World* CD, find a quiet moment to soak up God's message of love communicated through Marilyn Baker in her song *The Father's Song of Love.*

Since God has poured so much love into you, resolve to give love to others this Christmastime. If Christmas is a time of loneliness for you, this will take much grace. Ask God to give you that grace and to show you who would welcome a card, a phone-call, a letter or an invitation from you.

A Prayer

Lord Jesus,
Thank you that so often you choose to come to me through the expressed love of friends: through the warmth of their embrace; through the unexpected phone call; through the card arriving on the very day I needed encouragement. Although I know in my head that you love me always and that you even indwell me, I still need you to come to me through the warmth of a human hug, the tenderness of a gentle touch, the understanding of a loving look, the encouragement expressed through an e-mail, the affirmation of an appreciative 'Well done!' For every expression of your love, I thank you. May I, in turn, pour love into others.[4]

God,

grant us a glimpse of glory
in our homes,
Let us see that the love of our loved ones
is a reflection of your love.
As we are loved and cared for,
help us to care for all who are in need.
We pray for our places of work
and rest,
that they may be places of peace.
Mighty God, come to us
and give us your peace.[5]

Chapter Ten

In 'the Poor'

More and more Christians are discovering the joy that comes through caring for 'the poor' at Christmas-time. By 'the poor' I am not thinking only of the homeless or the penniless, though they are included in the term, of course. I also mean the lonely, the sick, the bereaved, those who are separated from their loved ones at this time of year.

I well remember, for example, the joy that filled me one Christmas morning when I attended the Communion Service at the hospital where I had been a patient earlier in the year. Now that I was fit and well, I had the privilege of taking present patients by wheelchair to the chapel that had been an oasis for me while I was recovering from surgery. God came to me that morning in the looks of gratitude the patients gave me as we travelled in the lift together. Those looks were more priceless than any gift that money can buy. As I write, I am preparing to leave for a month-long trip to Singapore. There I shall meet with many men and women who, when they were students here in England, used to spend Christmas with our family. On those occasions our home was not only filled with chaos but with love and laughter as well. It was filled, too, with worship as we ended the day with carol singing, and read of that glorious day when people of all nations will worship the King who came to us as a child.

Jean Vanier, lover and champion of the poor and founder of the L'Arche communities for people with mental handicaps writes:

Christians have always proclaimed
the need to serve the poor,
to do things that will help them
rise up out of their misery.
But what we are discovering at l'Arche
is that those who are poor possess a precious gift
and that we must listen to them with deep respect.
They have a gift for others.
We are discovering too
that the life-giving Jesus is hidden in them.
He is truly there.
If you become a friend of the poor,
You become a friend of Jesus . . .
'If you enter into a close relationship with those who are
     poor,
you enter into an intimate relationship with Jesus.'[1]

He goes on to quote from Matthew 25:31ff:

'When he finally arrives, blazing in beauty and all his angels with him, the Son of Man will take his place on his glorious throne. Then all the nations will be arranged before him and he will sort the people out, much as a shepherd sorts out sheep and goats, putting sheep to his right and goats to his left.

'Then the King will say to those on his right, "Enter, you who are blessed by my Father! Take what's coming to you in this kingdom. It's been ready for you since the world's foundation. And here's why:

> *I was hungry and you fed me,*
> *I was thirsty and you gave me a drink,*
> *I was homeless and you gave me a room,*
> *I was shivering and you gave me clothes,*
> *I was sick and you stopped to visit,*
> *I was in prison and you came to me."*

'Then those "sheep" are going to say, "Master, what are you talking about? When did we ever see you hungry and feed you, thirsty and give you a drink? And when did we ever see you sick or in prison and come to you?" Then the King will say, "I'm telling the solemn truth: Whenever you did one of these things to someone overlooked or ignored, that was me – you did it to me." '

(Mt 25:31–40 The Message)

Jean Vanier reflects, as many of us have reflected:

It seems so impossible that the Father should be revealed in the anguished face of a child.
Who is this God
Who resides in the broken heart[2]

A Response

When asked by Malcolm Muggeridge to make a television programme about her work in Calcutta, Mother Teresa reluctantly agreed with this now-famous phrase: 'Well, let's do something beautiful for God!'

Ask God to show you if there is something beautiful you can do for him this Christmas.

When Mother Teresa and her Sisters scooped up the dying from the streets of Calcutta, they nursed each person as though he or she were Jesus. Ask Jesus for the grace this Christmas to serve those around you as though you were serving him.

If you have the *Joy to the World* CD, listen to the hymn, *Brother, Sister Let Me Serve You.*

Cut out from a newspaper or magazine pictures of 'the poor' who are in the news. Pray for them now.

A Hymn

Brother, sister, let me serve you,
Let me be as Christ to you;
Pray that I may have the grace
To let you be my servant, too.

We are pilgrims on a journey,
Fellow trav'llers on the road;
We are here to help each other
Walk the mile and bear the load.

I will hold the Christlight for you
In the night-time of your fear;
I will hold my hand out to you,
Speak the peace you long to hear.

I will weep when you are weeping;
When you laugh, I'll laugh with you.
I will share your joy and sorrow
Till we've seen this journey through.

When we sing to God in heaven,
We shall find such harmony,
Born of all we've known together
Of Christ's love and agony.[3]

A Prayer

God of the poor,
We long to meet you
Yet we almost miss you;
We strive to help you
Yet only discover our need.
Interrupt our comfort
With your nakedness,
Touch our possessiveness
With your poverty,
And surprise our guilt
With the grace of your welcome
In Jesus Christ. Amen[4]

Christmas Poor

You are the caller,
You are the poor
You are the stranger
        At my door
You are the wanderer
    The unfed
You are the homeless
        With no bed
You are the man
        Driven insane
You are the child
        Crying in pain
You are the other
        Who comes to me
If I open to another
        You're born in me.[5]

Chapter Eleven

In Silence

Silent night! Holy night!
All is calm, all is bright,
Round yon virgin, mother and child,
Holy Infant, so tender and mild,
Sleep in heavenly peace,
Sleep in heavenly peace.

Silent night! Holy night!
Son of God, love's pure light;
Radiant beams Thy holy face
With the dawn of redeeming grace,
Jesus, Lord at Thy birth
Jesus, Lord at Thy birth.[1]

That must be one of the world's favourite carols. Many of us, too, love the part of the Midnight Service of Holy Communion where we remind one another that:

> *While all things were in **quiet silence**, and night was in the*
> *midst of her swift course,*
> *Your almighty Word, O Lord, leaped down out of your royal*
> *throne. Alleluia!*

Yes. We sing about silence and we speak about silence but, as Christmas Day comes close, the Martha in us takes control and we find ourselves busy, busy, busy like tops that cannot stop spinning.

Nevertheless, God continues to woo us away from the hectic schedules we set ourselves to: 'Be still, and know that I am God' (Ps 46:10).

God wants us to be so still that we can enjoy intimacy with him.

Although that invitation may seem irrelevant at this time of year, the curious thing is that when we take the invitation seriously and take time out to do as God asks, we find that we achieve more and not less. There are many reasons for this. One is that priorities are most clearly discovered when we are still rather than when we are living life at top speed. Another is that our energy levels that are sorely depleted by rush and bustle are topped up when we pause to be still. A third reason is that, when we are still before God, we know ourselves loved. This love motivates us to return to the melee to give of our energies and love once more. Author Bill Volkman describes how this happened for him:

> *Most of my life I have been a compulsive, helter-skelter doer*
> *– and always in a hurry.*
>
> *I had never taken much time to bask in anyone or*
> *anything. I needed to learn to ask less and to bask more. I*
> *needed to wrestle less and nestle more; to struggle less and*
> *snuggle more . . .*[2]

As he learned the art of becoming still once, then twice each day, he discovered the joy of basking 'in the presence of my indwelling Lover' and anticipating 'the healing power and transformation that flows to anyone who reaches out in faith to touch Jesus'.[3]

Bill Volkman's experience can be ours also – even at this time of year. All it needs is the resolve to create a few minutes when we can come before God and let go of all the tension that drains us, the questions that pester us and the plans that drive us; to tune in to the presence and love of the One whose birthday we celebrate on Christmas Day. He longs to love us, to enrich us, to strengthen us, to guide us. Our role is to let it happen – to allow him to love us and speak to us.

A Resolve

Try to find a place where you can be still for a few minutes most days:

> There should be at least a room, or some corner where no one will find you and disturb you or notice you. You should be able to untether yourself from the world and set yourself free, loosing all the fine strings and strands of tension that bind you, by sight, by sound, by thought, to the presence of others.[4]

Not everyone has such a place but a woman I once met told me that she finds space and stillness like that while watching television! 'When the commercials are on, I close my eyes and tune into Jesus. My husband thinks I'm asleep, but I'm not. I'm praying'. Another woman uses a fitted wardrobe as a prayer place. Where there's a will there's a way!

Read this version of Psalm 23 as slowly as you can, pausing when a word or a phrase or a sentence makes an impact on you.

The Lord is My Pace-Setter

The Lord is my Pace-setter, I shall not rush
He makes me stop and rest for quiet intervals.
He provides me with images of stillness
Which restore my serenity
He leads me in ways of efficiency through
calmness of mind and His guidance is peace.
Even though I have a great many things to
accomplish each day
I will not fret
For His presence is there.
His timelessness, His all-importance,
Will keep me in balance.
He prepares refreshment and renewal
In the midst of my activity
By anointing my mind with His oils of
tranquillity
My cup of joyous energy overflows.
Surely harmony and effectiveness
Shall be the fruits of my hours,
For I shall walk in the pace of my Lord
And dwell in His house for ever.[5]

Ask God to give you the grace to allow him to set the pace
for you.

If you have a CD or cassette with the carol *Silent Night* on it, or if you have the *Joy to the World* CD, listen to that carol from time to time. Let it calm you. Or pray this prayer which also features on the CD that accompanies this book:

Calm me, Lord, as you calmed the storm;
Still me, Lord, keep me from harm.
Let all the tumult within me cease,
Enfold me, Lord, in your peace.[6]

Now, hand the pressures over to God and soak up his peace asking yourself:

Do I need
to ask less
and to bask more?
To struggle less
and
to snuggle more?

If the answer is yes, what are you going to do about it?

Be silent.
Be still.
Alone. Empty
before your God.
Say nothing.
Ask nothing.
Be silent.
Be still.
Let your God
look upon you.
That is all.
He knows.
He understands.
He loves you with
an enormous love.
He only wants to
look upon you
with his love.
Quiet.
Still.
Be.
Let your God —
love you.[7]

Blue Tit

Chapter Twelve

In Nature

'The Lord *will* return.' That's the message that fills countless Christians with joy, excitement and anticipation throughout this Advent season. 'The Lord is here. By his Spirit he's with us. Now!' This paradox challenges us at this time of year too. As we have already seen, because both of these claims are true, we not only wait for Jesus to return in glory, we can experience him in the middle of the bustle and busyness of this so-called 'holy season'. As Ernest Boyer puts it in *Finding God at Home*:

> Jesus proclaimed the 'already' of the Christian message . . . he also proclaimed the 'not yet' . . . God is fully present, God has still more to give. But of the two it is the 'already' that Christians most often forget . . . never seeking to discover its full meaning in their lives. And yet this 'already' can never be known through simple words . . . it must be felt.[1]

Jesus reminded us that one way we can tune into, see, sense and feel God's presence is through contemplating the wonders of his creation. I write today to the accompaniment of the chirping of a blue-tit and the call of a wood pigeon. This music reminds me of Jesus' suggestion that we listen to the language of his creation:

> *'Don't worry about everyday life – whether you have enough food, drink, and clothes. Doesn't life consist of more than food and clothing? Look at the birds. They don't need to plant or harvest or put food in barns because your heavenly Father feeds them. And you are far more valuable to him than they are . . .'*
>
> (Mt 6:26 NLT)

Commenting on this passage, John Stott writes:

> It was Jesus Christ himself in the Sermon on the Mount who told us to be bird-watchers! 'Behold the fowls of the air' is how the King James' Version renders his command (Matthew 6:26). Translated into basic English, however, his instruction becomes 'watch birds!' So we have the highest possible authority for this activity. Moreover, he meant more than that we should notice them. For the Greek verb employed here means to fix the eyes on or take a good look at. This will certainly include our study and appreciation of their plumage and behaviour. But the Bible tells us that birds have lessons to teach us as well.[2]

Joni Eareckson Tada the now-famous author, speaker and singer reminds us of a day when God spoke eloquently to her through bird watching. Having been in a wheelchair for twenty-five years after breaking her neck in a diving accident, she began to suffer from other health problems. In an effort to cheer her up, her husband hung a bird feeder outside her

window. At first, she found herself envying the freedom these
birds enjoyed. Suddenly, though, she recalled what Jesus said
about sparrows: 'Not even a sparrow, worth only half a penny,
can fall to the ground without your Father knowing it. And the
very hairs on your head are all numbered. So don't be afraid;
you are more valuable to him than a whole flock of sparrows'
(Mt 10:29 NLT).

> I glanced at the bird feeder and smiled [Joni writes]. I
> could understand Jesus noticing an eagle . . . But a
> scrappy Sparrow? They're a dime a dozen. Jesus said so
> himself. Yet from thousands of bird species the Lord
> chose the most insignificant, least-noticed, scruffiest bird
> of all. A pint-sized thing that even dedicated birdwatchers
> ignore. That thought alone calmed my fears. I felt
> significant and noticed . . . If the great God of heaven
> concerns himself with a ragtag little Sparrow clinging to
> the bird feeder outside my window, he cares about you.[3]

Jesus not only encouraged us to gaze at birds, he begs us to
contemplate wildflowers also:

> *'Instead of looking at the fashions, walk out into the fields
> and look at the wildflowers. They never primp or shop, but
> have you ever seen colour and design quite like it? The ten
> best-dressed men and women in the country look shabby
> alongside them.*
>
> *'If God gives such attention to the appearance of
> wildflowers – most of which are never even seen – don't you
> think he'll attend to you, take pride in you, do his best for
> you?'*
>
> (Mt 6:28,29 The Message)

A Response

Take a few minutes today to gaze at birds clustered round a bird feeder or hopping round the garden. Or take a leisurely look at a poinsettia, some winter pansies, some holly berries or other plants or flowers. Ask yourself four questions if you have time:

What is God saying through this little piece of his vast creation?
What is God saying to *me*?
Just supposing I could *become* that bird or plant, how might I feel?
What do *I* want to say to God or do for God in response to what I have seen or heard or felt?

* * *

Read the following piece from Psalm 19 and resolve to look up more regularly – to enjoy the sunrise and the sunset and the spectacular sight of a full moon or a star-studded sky:

> The heavens tell of the glory of God.
> The skies display his marvellous craftsmanship.
> Day after day they continue to speak;
> night after night they make him known.
> They speak without a sound or a word;
> their voice is silent in the skies;
> yet their message has gone out to all the earth,
> And their words to all the world.
>
> (Psalm 19:1–4 NLT)

Now, if you have the *Joy to the World* CD, listen to the hymn: *How Great Thou Art*, especially verse 1.

Ponder the truths spelt out in this Drama of Creation:

In the beginning, God made the world:
Made it and mothered it,
Shaped it and fathered it;
Filled it with seed and with signs of fertility,
Filled it with life and with song and variety.
All that is green, blue, deep and growing,
All that is tender, firm, fragrant and curious,
All that crawls, flies, swims, walks
or is motionless,
All that speaks, sings, cries, laughs or keeps silence,
All that suffers, lacks, limps or longs for an end,
God's is the hand that created you.
The world belongs to God,
The Earth and all its people.[4]

*Listen to the song of heaven and nature today – and **enjoy!***

Chapter Thirteen

In Our Preparations

I find it fascinating to unearth ways in which Christians down the ages and from different walks of life prepare to celebrate Christmas. Last year, for example, I looked up the word Advent on the Internet and discovered how many Americans prepare their hearts to celebrate the birth of the Saviour of the World: 'Candles in the window, a wreath on the door, mistletoe hung high, poinsettias aflame with brilliant colour, gifts beneath a lighted tree, friends around a holiday table, families reunited in love, church bells ringing . . . This is Christmas in America!' one writer claimed.

One of my favourite stories about Christmas preparations, though, stems from the thirteenth century and centres around an initiative taken by St Francis. Near the hermitage in the Italian village of Greccio where Francis lived towards the end of his life was a cave that was very similar to the grotto in Bethlehem where it is believed that Jesus was born. One

Christmas Francis found himself longing that he and his fellow villagers would experience what God did for us in giving us his one and only Son. To achieve this aim, he decided to turn 'his' cave into the kind of stable where he believed Jesus was born. He shared his vision with the lord of Greccio and asked him to have a manger built, to fill it with straw and hay and have it placed in the cave. He also asked his aristocratic friend to send animals to the cave: an ass, some oxen and some sheep. These were to stand either side of the manger. At midnight on Christmas Eve, they would have a celebration of Holy Communion using the manger as the holy table.

Meanwhile, invitations to come to the cave at midnight were sent to each of the peasants in the valley, all the hillmen of the small towns that looked down on Greccio and every brother in each of the hermitages. They came. Some carried flaming torches, others brought candles, many sang hymns and carols. 'The forest resounded with their voices,' recalls Bonaventura, a Companion of St Francis. 'And that memorable night was made glorious by many brilliant lights and psalms of praise.'

Francis radiated deep-down joy. One version of the story claims that, during the service, with the animals standing by, the priest placed the bread and the wine on the straw and all the people sank to their knees in wonder, love and praise. There in the cave, they sensed the presence of Emmanuel – God with us: God lying in the straw in the form of bread and wine.

Another version of the story claims that, when the villagers arrived, they saw by the light of their torches, a baby lying in the manger, wrapped in strips of cloth. He was kept warm by the steamy breath of the farm animals. Francis stood close to the manger overcome with love – enraptured. Meanwhile, a member of the 'congregation' was given a vision of a lifeless baby lying in a manger. In the vision, Francis went to the child and touched him. The child woke up 'as from a deep sleep'. The crowd understood immediately what the vision meant.

Jesus had been forgotten by many of the villagers but, through this 'nativity play', Francis had rekindled in the hearts of those among whom he lived, a heart-love for the child of Bethlehem.

The story reminds me of an occasion when I was visiting a friend in hospital. It was Christmas Eve. After I'd given my friend a farewell kiss and a small Christmas gift, I wandered into the hospital chapel to pray. A nun was there. Quietly and prayerfully she was putting in place the Christmas crib – re-enacting in her own way the tradition St Francis unwittingly started. The way she arranged the shepherds and their sheep, the oxen and the manger, filled me with a sense of awe and wonder that resolved into heart adoration and worship. On this occasion *I* was the one who tuned afresh into the presence of Emmanuel, God with us, in such a way that I could do nothing but gasp in wonder, love and praise

For Reflection

This Christmas, can you think of a way of communicating without words the kind of joy that St Francis communicated to the villagers among whom he lived? Perhaps you could place in your home a crib or a card with a nativity scene on it, an Advent candle or calendar or some other visual centre-piece that helps you and others to enter into the awesomeness of the good news that God spells out so joyfully through the prophet Isaiah:

The people who walked in darkness
have seen a great light.
They lived in a land of shadows,
but now light is shining on them.
You have given them great joy, Lord;
You have made them happy.
They rejoice in what you have done,
as people rejoice when they harvest
their corn . . .

For a child is born to us!
*   A son is given to us! . . .*
He will be called, 'Wonderful Counsellor',
*   'Mighty God,'*
*   'Eternal Father,'*
*   'Prince of Peace.'*
His royal power will continue to grow.

(Is 9:2,3,6,7a GNB)

A Prayer

Pray that those who come into your home this Christmas may
be touched by the light of Christ – maybe through your crib or
candle, Advent calendar or candle – or because you yourself are
aglow with a quiet joy that communicates in a way that you will
never understand.

At this feast of the Nativity
Let each person
Wreathe the door of his heart
So that the Holy Spirit
May delight in his door,
Enter in
And take up residence there;
Then by the Spirit
He will be made holy.[1]

Preparing for Christmas

Such a flurry of excitement
seemed to fill the air in town today, Lord.
Women hurried through the bazaar
clutching poinsettias and Christmas cakes
and tinsel to hang on Christmas trees.
Men puffed and panted and heaved and sighed
as they persuaded huge evergreens
into their pre-Christmas show-places –
outside offices and shops and public buildings.

Father Christmas appeared too
as though from nowhere –
still clutching his customary dove,
still gazing at the fairy lights that straddle the streets
and twinkle above the shoppers.
I became part of the euphoria, Lord.
I also clutched my poinsettia
and tinsel,
pine cones sprayed with silver,
red candles and scarlet ribbons.

'But what are they celebrating?', I wonder.
What am I?
You came.
You continue to come.
You will come again.
That's it in a nutshell.
That's the cause of my celebration
And joy.[2]

He Comes

Chapter Fourteen

Through Angels

God comes to us in a variety of ways, as we have seen over the past few days. Anyone who takes seriously the stories surrounding God's preparation for the entry into the world of his Son cannot deny the existence and involvement of angels.

Angels, according to the author of the letter to the Hebrews, are 'spirits in the service of God, commissioned to serve the heirs of God's salvation' (Heb 1:14 JBP). Myriads of these exotic, glorious, non-material beings shuttle through the pages of the Bible fulfilling their ambassadorial role. They offer guidance and give specific instructions to humans. As God explained to Moses:

> *'See, I am sending my angel before you to lead you safely to the land I have prepared for you. Pay attention to him, and obey all of his instructions . . .'*
>
> (Ex 23:20–21 NLT)

They protect and deliver God's people:

> *The angel of the LORD guards all who fear him, and he rescues them.*
>
> (Ps 34:7 NLT)

In other words, angels are divine beings appointed by God to be extensions of his right hand. We see angels playing a major role

I am Gabriel, the sentinel of God

in paving the way for the conception of both John the Baptist and Jesus. Luke recalls the day when the elderly, prayerful priest Zechariah was visited by one of these heavenly ambassadors. In the course of his priestly duties, Zechariah had entered the Holy of Holies in the temple in Jerusalem. He was about to burn incense and to pray, on behalf of the people of Israel, that God would send the promised Messiah when, 'Unannounced, an angel of God appeared just to the right of the altar of incense. Zachariah was paralyzed in fear' (Lk 1:11 The Message).

It would appear that Zechariah had added a personal prayer to the national one. His wife had suffered the heartache and stigma of childlessness for many, many years. And like Abraham of old, it would appear that Zechariah pleaded with God for the gift of a child. Luke takes up the story:

> *But the angel reassured him, 'Don't fear, Zachariah. Your prayer has been heard. Elizabeth, your wife, will bear a son by you. You are to name him John. You're going to leap like a gazelle for joy, and not only you – many will delight in his birth. He'll achieve great stature with God.*
>
> *He'll drink neither wine nor beer. He'll be filled with the Holy Spirit from the moment he leaves his mother's womb. He will turn many sons and daughters of Israel back to their God. He will herald God's arrival in the style and strength of Elijah, soften the hearts of parents to children, and kindle devout understanding among hardened skeptics – he'll get the people ready for God.'*
>
> *Zachariah said to the angel, 'Do you expect me to believe this? I'm an old man and my wife is an old woman.'*
>
> *But the angel said, 'I am Gabriel, the sentinel of God, sent especially to bring you this glad news. But because you won't believe me, you'll be unable to say a word until the day of your son's birth. Every word I've spoken to you will come true on time – God's time . . .'*
>
> *Meanwhile, the congregation waiting for Zachariah*

was getting restless, wondering what was keeping him so long in the sanctuary. When he came out and couldn't speak, they knew he had seen a vision. He continued speechless and had to use sign language with the people.

When the course of his priestly assignment was completed, he went back home. It wasn't long before his wife, Elizabeth, conceived.

(Lk 1:12–25 The Message)

A Response

If you were in a special prayer place today and you could ask God for whatever you want, what would you ask for? You *are* in a special place because, in the economy of God, every place can become a holy place just as any bush can become a burning bush. So make your request to God now bearing in mind the way Zephaniah describes God's feeling, not just for Jerusalem, but for us also:

The Lord your God has arrived . . .
He will rejoice over you in great gladness;
He will love you and not accuse you.
Is that a joyous choir I hear? No,
It is the LORD himself exulting over you in a happy song.
(Zeph 3:17 LB)

The angel's prophecy concerning John the Baptist was fulfilled. John goes down in history as the man who prepared people to receive Jesus and his teaching. How would you like to go down in history?

*   *   *

John fulfilled his God-given mission with the help of the Holy Spirit. Ask for a fresh touch of God's Spirit for yourself today.

When Elizabeth discovered that, against all the odds, she was pregnant, she was overwhelmed: 'How kind the Lord is!' she exclaimed. 'He has taken away my disgrace of having no children!' (Lk 1:25 NLT). As you look back over another year, can you detect evidence of the kindness of God in your life? If so, thank him now for specific kindnesses that come to mind.

Gaze at the glorious picture of the angel that illustrates today's meditation and ponder the mysteries the Psalmist spells out:

The angel of the Lord guards and rescues all who fear him
(Ps. 34:7 NRSV)

A Prayer

Blessed are you, Lord Jesus Christ.
You came down and took upon you our humanity,
That you might raise us up to share in your divinity.

By the obedience of Mary,
Lord made flesh

Dwell among us.

By the understanding of Joseph,
Lord made flesh

Dwell among us.

By the song of the angels,
Lord made flesh

Dwell among us.

By your birth in a manger,
    Lord made flesh

Dwell among us.

By the adoration of the shepherds,
    Lord made flesh

Dwell among us.

By the worship of the wise men,
    Lord made flesh

Dwell among us.[1]

Chapter Fifteen

As The Holy Spirit

Six months after the angel Gabriel appeared to Zechariah, we find him visiting a young woman who was probably still in her teens. We know little about Mary apart from the fact that she was engaged to a carpenter called Joseph and that she lived in the tiny town of Nazareth that nestled on the slopes of Lower Galilee.

Luke describes how Gabriel encountered Mary:

'Greetings, favoured woman! The Lord is with you!'

Confused and disturbed, Mary tried to think what the angel could mean. 'Don't be frightened, Mary,' the angel told her, 'for God has decided to bless you! You will become pregnant and have a son, and you are to name him Jesus. He will be very great and will be called the Son of the Most High. And the Lord God will give him the throne of his ancestor David. And he will reign over Israel forever; his Kingdom will never end!'

Mary asked the angel, 'But how can I have a baby? I am a virgin.'

The angel replied, 'The Holy Spirit will come upon you, and the power of the Most High will overshadow you. So the baby born to you will be holy, and he will be called the Son of God . . .'

> *Mary responded, 'I am the Lord's servant, and I am*
> *willing to accept whatever he wants. May everything you*
> *have said come true.' And then the angel left.*
>
> (Lk 1:28b–35; 38 NLT)

This passage throbs with the thrilling news that the Creator of the universe seeks the co-operation of an ordinary young woman when he seeks to break into the history of the world he himself had created. The passage pulsates, too, with the equally thrilling message that, when a human being says 'Yes' to God, by the peculiar power of the Holy Spirit, he or she can change and be changed. This passage proclaims the almost unbelievable news that, by the overshadowing and ministry of God's Spirit, a young virgin becomes 'the selfless space where God becomes man'.

I sometimes attempt to slip myself into Mary's sandals; to imagine how it might have felt suddenly to become aware that she had an angel by her side. One such occasion was particularly powerful. By my side I could see a bright light and feel a strange warmth. The sense of the holiness of God was so strong that I knelt on the floor and buried my head in my hands. When the angel whispered that I had found favour with God, my heart glowed. 'This is really all I want from him – to please him, to serve him', I wrote later. The light and the warmth of the divine presence lingered long after I sensed that the angel had departed. I sat down, cupped my hands and prayed, 'Come, Holy Spirit.' As I rested, I was aware that, somehow, the Spirit of God was at work in me and sensed that I had caught a glimpse of how he might have worked in Mary. As she moved from the question: 'Me?' to 'How?' and on to the answer: 'Yes', the Creator Spirit planted within her womb the divine seed. From that moment, God's Son, the Christ-child, nestled and grew inside her. The entire process was laced with peace and gentleness.

Sometime later, I felt moved when I came across this prayer:

I am the Lord, your Saviour . . .
I want you to enter into my love.
Yes, I want you to come so close to me that
I can speak my love into your heart.

I want to come to you as I came to Mary.
I look on you as I looked on Mary.

I am not looking at your greatness
nor at your attempts at asserting yourself
or trying to stand out from others.
I see your littleness
I see deep within you –
behind all your various disguises,
masks and roles –
I see the child,
My beloved child who is hungry and cries
for My love.
Come to Me.
Rest in Me.
Stay with Me . . .
I am the Lord, your Saviour.
I want to come to you now and enfold you with my love
on all sides.

I do not want to drill My love into your life.
I want to bring it to birth in you.
Mary's task is yours too.
To receive Jesus into your life and to bring
My love to birth into your world.
In that way I can use you as a channel
for My love.

Through you I can love the people I send
across your path.

I can use your eyes to look at them
with my goodness.
I can use your ears to listen to them.
I can use your mouth to speak to them.

Rest now in my Love.
Then I can do great things for you too,
And through you.[1]

* * *

We cannot do great things for God without the enabling of the third person of the Trinity, the Holy Spirit. *With* the Holy Spirit, though, we can change and be changed. The Holy Spirit's ministry, among other things, is 'to make us holy, by making us know and feel the reality of God through his Son Jesus Christ.'[2] One of the ways in which the Holy Spirit achieves this miracle is by giving us the grace to discover, encounter and have fellowship with Emmanuel who is not only God with us but God *in* us. Another of the tasks of the Holy Spirit is to spread deep inside us the love of God so that we know that we are precious in God's sight. God's love for us, in-breathed by his Holy Spirit enables us to enjoy an intimacy with God that is life-changing.

A Response

Mary's response to the visit of the angel was: '*My soul is full of joy in God my Saviour*' (Lk 1:47 JBP).

'A happiness of the heart', that's how one author defines joy adding: 'The word covers the entire spectrum of what may be called the rapturous, ranging from the extreme achings of ecstasy to the quiet thrill of contentment.'[3]

'Delight', 'exultation', 'exhilaration' are words other people have used to try to sum up 'joy'.

What words you use to describe any joy you feel as Christmas approaches?

Listen to the following invitation from God if you have the *Joy to the World* CD. If you do not have the CD or cassette, simply read the words and relax.

An Invitation From God

Rest in my love
Relax in my care
And know that my presence
Will always be there
You are my child
And I care for you
There's nothing My love and
My power cannot do.

Jesus is here
He is alive
And all power is given unto Him
His peace and joy
He gives to you
Brings strength and comfort to your heart.[4]

A Prayer to the Holy Spirit

Holy Spirit,
source of all truth,
giver of power
Come upon me now
As gently as a dove
Or like tongues of living fire
As quietly as a summer breeze
Or as a mighty roaring wind.
Come and dwell within me.
Enable me now to do those things
Which before were impossible.
Unworthy as I am,
Holy Spirit of the living God
Give me those gifts which I can use
To your honour and glory
That I may show forth your fruit
Even in my life.
Glory be to you Father
Glory be to you Lord Jesus Christ
Glory be to you Holy Spirit.

Amen.[5]

Chapter Sixteen

Through Friends

Was Mary ever tempted to believe that the angel's visit had been nothing more than a memorable dream? We are not told. What we are told is that very soon after she had received the news that she was to be the mother of the Messiah, she hurried away from Nazareth and made the eighty-mile trip to Judaea to visit her cousin Elizabeth. If she was harbouring doubts about the reality of the angel's message or wondering whether she really was pregnant, her doubts were quickly dispelled by the gracious greeting Elizabeth gave her:

> *With little delay Mary got ready and hurried off to the hillside town in Judaea where Zacharias and Elisabeth lived. She went into their house and greeted her cousin. When Elizabeth heard her greeting, the unborn child stirred inside her and she herself was filled with the Holy Spirit, and cried out, 'Blessed are you among women, and blessed is your child! What an honour it is to have the mother of my Lord come to see me! Why, as soon as your greeting reached my ears, the child within me jumped for joy! Oh, how happy is the woman who believes in God, for he does make his promises to her come true.*

(Lk 1:39–45 JBP)

God so often speaks to us through other people – especially our close friends. On this occasion, he chose Elizabeth to confirm the angel's message and to testify to the fact that Mary was, indeed, pregnant by the Holy Spirit. Mary's response was one of overflowing love laced with awe and wonder and pure, uninhibited joy:

> *Then Mary said, 'My heart is overflowing with praise of my Lord, my soul is full of joy in God my Saviour. For he has deigned to notice me, his humble servant and, after this, all the people who ever shall be will call me the happiest of women! The One who can do all things has done great things for me – oh, holy is his Name! Truly, His mercy rests on those who fear Him in every generation . . .'*
>
> (Lk 1:46–54 JBP)

God gave Mary and Elizabeth to one another at a time when both were particularly vulnerable. Elizabeth had long borne the stigma 'the barren one' because she was childless. Now, although humanly speaking she was beyond the age of child-bearing, suddenly she was pregnant! Mary, on the other hand, had suddenly become an unmarried mother in an age and culture where pre-marital pregnancy was so scandalous that it was punishable by death. Together, these two happily bewildered women enjoyed the luxury of three months together when they could rejoice with each other in the pure generosity and goodness of God.

A Response

Think of a time when you have felt vulnerable and when God has given you a friend with whom you can share freely and without inhibition. Then read and ponder the following claims:

The love we share in human relationships is part of the grandness of a God who cradles us tenderly in his all-loving embrace. Whenever pure, selfless love is shared, we

experience God.[1]

God uses our human relationships to reach us; we experience him loving and being loved by another. God reveals himself to us in the real life presence of those around us.[2]

The intimacy between people that results from unselfish love is also the intimacy with Father, Son and Spirit that is the life of grace.[3]

True friendship is mystery. It takes us in and captures us. We do not analyze it, but live within it and experience its fullness. It has a quality that speaks to the very core of a person about the sweetness and beauty of God. True friendship is inexorably linked to God.[4]

Thank God for this friendship, his faithfulness and that he fills our emptiness with his fullness in a whole variety of ways. Light a candle to remind you of the warmth of the friendship that you have enjoyed then join Mary in her song of praise – listening to it, perhaps, on the *Joy to the World* CD.

My soul proclaims the greatness of the Lord,
And my spirit exults in God my Saviour
For he has looked with mercy on my lowliness
And his name shall be for ever exalted.
For the mighty One has done great things for me
And his mercy shall reach from age to age.
And holy, holy, holy
Is his name.

A Prayer

O Holy Spirit
You draw us like a magnet
not to yourself
but to Jesus
and to one another.
You gave Mary to Elizabeth
And Elizabeth to Mary
Enriching each through the other.
By grace, you brought joy into my life
Through . . . .
You impregnated us with your Spirit
Granting a friendship that has brought
Healing
Peace
And a taste of your love

Thank you

Chapter Seventeen

Through Worship

L ast Christmas I read the astonishing account of a miracle that took place in France during the First World War. A famous Canadian regiment had been sent to France to aid the British in their war against Germany. Since their lieutenant was a musician, the Canadians had taken a piano with them. Among other things, the lieutenant had used it to compose the famous war-time song *Mademoiselle from Armentiers.*

Christmas Eve came. The regiment was hiding in the front-line trenches close to the place where enemy troops were also hiding. They were so close that the voices of the German troops could be clearly heard. Curiously, the Canadians had carried the piano into the trenches.

Just before midnight, the lieutenant did a daring thing. He sat at the piano and started to play Christmas carols. First he played, *Silent Night, Holy Night.* The Canadian soldiers sang lustily. To their astonishment, within minutes, their enemies joined in by singing *their* version of the carol: *Stille Nacht, Heilige Nacht.* Several carols later, the lieutenant played a German aria from Wagner's *Tannhauser* whereupon a Canadian soldier scrambled out of his trench, stood in the open and sang.

'Mehr! Mehr!' (More! More!) the Germans shrieked. One of their own soldiers then emerged from his trench, stood where he could easily have become a target for enemy rifles, and blended his beautiful baritone voice with that of the Canadian's.

Battle-weary Canadians and Germans alike then witnessed the miracle that, for this night at least, they could abandon their instruments of destruction and concentrate instead on celebrating together the most amazing event the world has ever witnessed: the entry into this world of the baby who was Christ the Lord.[1]

The story reminds me of an occasion when, one Christmas Eve, a friend and I were watching the televised service of Nine Lessons and Carols from King's College, Cambridge. My friend, I realised, had not attended church for years. As the choir sang the familiar carols, though, and we heard the readings from Genesis and the Prophets as well as the Gospels, I detected a winsomeness in my friend's response. By the end of the service this seemed to have turned into a longing that she put into words: 'I've really wanted to go to a Carol Service this year but the opportunity just doesn't seem to have presented itself.' Once again, it seemed as though, while people were engaged in worship, God had crept in.

Something similar seems to have happened when Mary visited Elizabeth shortly after she had received the news that she had been given the privilege of becoming the mother of the Messiah. No one knows precisely why she hurried off to visit her cousin at that time. Some believe that it might have been to avoid the inevitable gossip with which Nazareth would have been riddled when the scandalous news that she was pregnant but unmarried was gossiped about and spread around the town. Others believe that Mary was simply going with the cultural flow – visiting her elderly cousin out of care and courtesy now that Elizabeth's good news had been made public by the angel.

Whatever the reason for the visit, it seems probable that after Gabriel had left Mary she was filled with a mixture of emotions: awe at the thought that she had been chosen out of all the women in the land who longed to be the mother of the Messiah. Fear as she anticipated the ripples of reaction that would inevitably rock her relationships with family and friends.

Dread lest Joseph would doubt her word and integrity when she told him her news; the further dread that, as custom required, he would have her stoned to death for unfaithfulness.

If fears and dreads like these clamoured for attention as she travelled to Elizabeth, her cousin's warm welcome must have been music to her ears. Filled with the Holy Spirit, Elizabeth gave a glad cry and exclaimed:

> *'You are blessed by God above all other women, and your child is blessed. What an honour this is, that the mother of my Lord should visit me! When you came in and greeted me, my baby jumped for joy the instant I heard your voice! You are blessed, because you believed that the Lord would do what he said.'*

> (Lk 1:42b–45 NLT)

Elizabeth's expressed excitement seems to have allayed any fears that might have been plaguing Mary. Consequently she added her own worship song to the worship dance that the foetus who was to become John the Baptist performed in Elizabeth's womb and Elizabeth's own exuberant song of praise:

> *'Oh, how I praise the Lord.*
> *How I rejoice in God my Saviour!*
> *For he took notice of his lowly servant girl,*
> *and now generation after generation*
> *will call me blessed.*
> *For he, the Mighty One, is holy,*
> *and he has done great things for me . . .'*

> (Lk 1:46b–49 NLT)

For Reflection and Prayer

Spend some time today thanking God for the 'wonders of his grace' expressed in the gift to us of his one and only Son. As Elizabeth Ruth Obbard puts it, 'When we thank God, when we praise him, we make him present again in our lives. A heart full of song helps us to make God our centre [and] have him as our constant refrain.'[2]

If you have the *Joy to the World* CD listen to Mary's Song: *My Soul Proclaims the Greatness of the Lord*. If you do not have the CD, re-read Mary's song from Luke 1:46b–49 and rejoice. Ask God also to fill you with the kind of awe and wonder that Elizabeth expressed:

As the infant leapt with gladness
At the presence of the Word,
So Elizabeth, believing,
Knew the Mother of her Lord,
And in awe proclaimed her blessed
In the Wonder of her Child.[3]

* * *

Faithful God,
this Christmas
as I sing the familiar carols,
hear the familiar readings
and ponder familiar mysteries,
grant me the grace of pure worship —
that ability Mary had
of attributing to you your worth,
and your inestimable greatness.
Teach me reverence.
Restore to me the ability to express
the love for you that burns
deep down in my heart,
Your goodness to me is so great,
You are light in my darkness
hope in my despair
strength in my weakness
the shelter in life's storms
and Yes —
My Saviour.

Chapter Eighteen

Through His Son

God comes to us in a whole variety of ways: in people, in 'the poor', through nature, in silence, in the ordinary and in the extraordinary. The most amazing, extraordinary and mysterious way in which he has revealed himself so far has been through his one and only Son, 'the Word made flesh'. The writer of the Epistle to the Hebrews joyously announces this good news:

> *Long ago God spoke many times and in many ways to our ancestors through the prophets. But now in these final days, he has spoken to us through his Son . . . The Son reflects God's own glory, and everything about him represents God exactly.*

(Heb 1:1–3 NLT)

The radiance of God's glory reflected in the helplessness, dependency and vulnerability of a human baby? The flawless expression of the nature of God revealed in a child? These are deep mysteries. A bishop once helped to unravel these mysteries for me. He told me that he was about to take a trip to India to make a study of other religions. On his return, I asked him what he had learned. His eyes lit up as he replied, 'I've come back more excited about being a Christian than I've ever been. The Christian God is the only one who asks to be handled, held, caressed and loved.'

The radiance of God reflected in the helplessness of a human baby

When the time was right, God sent the Son.
Sent him and suckled him,
Reared him and risked him;
Filled him with laughter and tears and compassion,
Filled him with anger and love and devotion.
Unwelcomed child, refugee and runaway.

Christ is God's own Son.

The Word became flesh,
He lived among us, He was one of us.

Christ is God's own Son.[1]

* * *

William Barclay explains the reason why Jesus came to live among us:

It is the simple fact that [people] did not know what God was like until Jesus came. The Greeks thought of a passionless God, beyond all joy and sorrow, looking on [people] in calm unmoved detachment – no help there. The Jews thought of a demanding God, whose name was law and whose function was that of Judge – nothing but terror there. Jesus came to tell of a God who was love, and in staggered amazement [people] could only say, 'We never knew that God was like that.' One of the functions of the incarnation is to bring [us] the knowledge of God . . . The distant God is become near and the God we feared has become the lover of [our] souls.[2]

A Response

Think carefully about William Barclay's claim: '*Jesus came to tell of a God who was love*'. Think, too, about his other claim: '*In staggered amazement, people could only say, "We never knew that God was like that."*' Ask yourself the following questions:

- Do I know – deep down in my heart – that God loves me?
- Am I sure that the God who once seemed so distant is close to me?

If your answer to the first of these questions is 'Yes', spend a few minutes listening to the song *O Let the Son of God Enfold You* if you have the *Joy to the World* CD, or say the words of the chorus and do what it invites you to do:

> *O let the Son of God enfold you with His Spirit*
>   *and His love.*
> *Let Him fill your heart and satisfy your soul.*
> *O let Him have the things that hold you*
> *And His Spirit like a dove*
> *Will descend upon your life and make you whole.*[3]

If your answer to the second question is also 'Yes', use this verse from *Away in a Manger* as a prayer:

> Be near me, Lord Jesus; I ask Thee to stay
> Close by me for ever, and love me, I pray,
> Bless all the dear children in Thy tender care,
> And fit us for heaven to live with Thee there.

If your response to those two questions is 'No', turn this claim over and over in your mind:

There is nothing you can do to make
God love you less
There is nothing you can do to make
God love you more.[4]

Ask God to give you the grace this Christmas to understand
and sense and see and feel what one theologian described as the
deepest theological insight he had ever discovered namely,

Jesus loves me this I know
For the Bible tells me so.

For Prayer:

Jim Packer insists that, until we know in our hearts that we
are loved by God, we will not experience joy for:

'the experience of being loved is a fountain-head of joy'.[5]

Pray that this Christmas you may know in your heart that
you are uniquely loved by God:

God our beloved,
born of a woman's body,
you came that we might look upon you,
and handle you with our own hands.
May we so cherish one another in our bodies
that we may also be touched by you;
through the Word made flesh, Jesus Christ.[6]

Holy and Mysterious God,
as we await the birthday of your Son,
cause us to marvel at the mystery —
that the Creator of the universe emptied
himself of glory
and put on the form of a foetus.
Restore to us the desire to pause
the serenity to gaze
the ability to wonder at the spectacle before us:
the Christ-child —
the radiance of God's glory —
God made man
God in human form
begging to be touched
handled
seen
known
loved.
Give us the grace to love you more
that this Christmas the glow in our hearts
may bring joy to you,
Sacred Three
Holy Trinity
Father, Son and Holy Spirit.[7]

He Came Bringing Joy

Chapter Nineteen

To Joseph

How did Joseph feel, I wonder, when he held Jesus in his arms for the first time? Did he marvel that he had been given the privilege of acting as guardian to God's Son? Was he like the father of a newborn child who tried to capture for me the emotions he felt as he watched his first child being born? 'It was a miracle,' he recalled. 'Wonderful. This baby is God's baby. Now all I want to do is to be with them and to serve them.' Or did Joseph recall the roller-coaster year that had preceded the birth of the Saviour?

Luke doesn't tell us. What he does emphasise, though, is that Joseph was a 'just man' – that is a kind, tender, sensitive, merciful and godly person so his mind was almost certainly full of the longing to serve Mary and Jesus. What is equally probable is that his heart was full of gratitude to God for the way he had cautioned him not to break off his relationship with Mary though it seemed as though she must have committed adultery:

> *This is the story of the birth of the Messiah. Mary his mother*
> *was betrothed to Joseph; before their marriage she found that*
> *she was with child by the Holy Spirit. Being a man of*
> *principle, and at the same time wanting to save her from*
> *exposure, Joseph desired to have the marriage contract set*
> *aside quietly. He had resolved on this, when an angel of the*
> *Lord appeared to him in a dream. 'Joseph son of David,' said*
> *the angel, 'do not be afraid to take Mary home with you as*
> *your wife. It is by the Holy Spirit that she has conceived this*
> *child. She will bear a son; and you shall give him the name*
> *Jesus (Saviour), for he will save his people from their sins.'*
> *All this happened in order to fulfil what the Lord declared*
> *through the prophet: 'The virgin will conceive and bear a*
> *son, and he shall be called Emmanuel', a name which means*
> *'God is with us'. Rising from sleep Joseph did as the angel*
> *had directed him; he took Mary home to be his wife, but had*
> *no intercourse with her until her son was born. And he*
> *named the child Jesus.*
>
> (Mt 1:18–25 NEB)

In Palestine, at the time when these events took place, marriages took place in three well-spaced-out stages. First there was the stage of engagement. Often, as is still the case in some countries where arranged marriages are the norm, this stage was entered into while the couple were still children. They were chosen for one another by their parents who preferred to trust their own wisdom rather than the passion of young men and women where a choice as far-reaching as a marriage relationship was concerned.

The second stage of the marriage, betrothal, was entered into many years later if the girl was willing to go through with the marriage. Betrothal was absolutely binding. The couple was now known as man and wife even though they did not consummate the marriage at this stage. Betrothal could be terminated in one way only – by divorce.

Stage three was the marriage itself. Often this took place a year after the betrothal though there were times when the bridegroom brought forward the date of the marriage.

As Joseph watched Mary nurse her baby, did he recall the years of engagement and those early months of betrothal? Did memories of the bombshell that nearly broke up the relationship surge to the surface of his brain reminding him of the way he agonised over the news that this little baby now in his arms had been conceived? Possibly. Luke's account of the turmoil Joseph was in when Mary's pregnancy was discovered is so detailed that the only person who could have provided him with so much data was Joseph himself. If that is the case, it would appear that the details of the spin Joseph was in were etched on his heart and mind for ever.

His anguish had been understandable but heart-breaking. He loved Mary. He believed in her. When he discovered that she was pregnant, though, the only explanation that made any sense was that she had had an affair. Yet 'Mary, having an affair?' The idea seemed preposterous. In his eyes she was so through and through good that such a betrayal was unthinkable. Even so, her figure was living proof that she was, indeed, pregnant and this left him with no choice. He would have to divorce her (Deut 22:23,24). Before he fell asleep one memorable day while he agonised and puzzled over the dilemma that confronted him he became certain of just one thing. He would exercise compassion for Mary by simply writing her a letter of divorce and handing it to her quietly in the presence of two witnesses. This would be painful enough but it would be private and spare her a great deal of the shame she would suffer if he took the other option: to publicise her betrayal in such a way that she ran the risk of being stoned to death watched by a crowd of critical eyes.

A male Bible commentator has observed that 'no husband

could be expected to believe in the virgin conception unless the truth was revealed supernaturally'. Whether that shrewd observation is true or not, God in his compassion, chose a supernatural way of convincing Joseph that the father of Mary's unborn child was not another man but none other than the Holy Spirit. As Joseph held the Holy Spirit's baby in his arms that first Christmas Day, did he recall what the angel said to him in the dream that convinced him that he should marry Mary rather than divorce her:

> *Joseph, remember that you are a valued descendant of David and that this is the backcloth against which you must interpret my message.*
> *Believe that this foetus is holy because he was conceived by the Holy Spirit.*
> *Recognise that you have an important part to play in this drama. Just as earthly fathers are the ones to name their children after their birth you are the one who has been chosen to act as the father to this child. You are to name him Jesus. This child will save his people from their sins.*

Joseph was a devout Jew. He would have known the Scriptures and been well versed since childhood in the prophecies that foretold the coming of the Messiah. Did the penny drop for him during this dream or on waking? Did he become suddenly aware that these ancient prophecies were unfolding before his very eyes: a virgin, 'his' Mary, had conceived; the Holy Spirit was the father, the child was to be called Jesus – God saves.

From the way he acted when he woke up from his dream, it would appear that Joseph *was* aware that Mary's child was no ordinary baby but the fulfilment of the promise his people had been waiting for, praying for, watching for for centuries. Whether he realised the full implications of the angel's message or not, without further hesitation, he acted – marrying Mary at the earliest opportunity. Now, here he was holding God's Son in his very own arms.

The psalmist claims: '*You will show me the path of life; in Your presence is fullness of joy, at Your right hand there are pleasures for evermore*' (Ps 16:11 The Amplified Bible).

God had shown Joseph the path of life. Now, here he was not just in the presence of the Word made flesh, but enjoying the enviable privilege of holding God in human form. If he stopped to survey his surroundings and compared them with his home in Nazareth, he would have admitted that this current home was far from ideal and yet he could experience joy because Jesus was there. And God had revealed to him through the angel in his dream that he had much to give to the Christ-child.

A Response

Look at the picture of Joseph, Mary and Jesus on p.117. Recognise that the *three* are bound in a close, God-given relationship. Joseph is not standing by helplessly and hopelessly. He was as involved as a father can be at this stage of a child's development. This is how God planned it:

'[Mary] will bear a son' . . .   [Joseph] must name him Jesus –

that is, Joseph must fulfil the responsibilities an earthly father in the Middle East fulfilled at this time in history.

Many Christians admire, even revere Mary yet feel ambivalent about Joseph. In the light of what you have just read, how do *you* feel about Joseph? What can you learn from him?

Ask God for the grace to become more like the God-appointed, God-chosen foster father of his son as you read the following words of *Joseph's Song* by Michael Card. You can also *hear* this lovely song on Michael Card's album *The Life* (disk 1), published by Sparrow Records, 1988.

Joseph's Song

How could it be, this baby in my arms,
Sleeping now so peacefully,
The Son of God, the angel said,
How could it be?

Lord, I know, he's not my own,
Not of my flesh, not of my bone,
Still fatherless, this baby be,
The Son of my love.

Father, show me where I fit into this plan of yours,
How can a man be father to the Son of God?
Lord, for all my life, I've been a simple carpenter,
How can I raise a King, how can I raise a King?

He looks so small, his face and hands so fair.
And when he cries, the sun just seems to disappear,
But when he laughs, it shines again, how could it be?

Father, show me where I fit into this plan of yours,
How can a man be father to the Son of God?
Lord, for all my life I've been a simple carpenter,
How can I raise a King, How can I raise a King?

How could it be, this baby in my arms,
Sleeping now so peacefully,
The Son of God, the angel said,
How could it be? How could it be? [1]

Picture Joseph holding God's baby son as you use the following prayers:

Mysterious God,
You broke into Joseph's life
Prompted him to marry Mary
And to act as father to your Son.
Break into my life,
Open my eyes,
Unstop my ears
That I may receive your healing touch
Be shown where I have misinterpreted the past
And discern the way ahead you have prepared for me.
Give me the grace you granted Joseph —
To tread your path willingly,
Patiently and persistently,
Whatever the cost
And to discover again that
In your presence is fullness of joy.

* * *

Into our world of darkness,
Into our places of strife,
Into our troubles and weakness,
Come, Lord.
Come down, come in, come among us.

Into our joys and celebrations,
Into our homes and to our loved ones,
Into our work and our achievements,

Come, Lord.
Come down, come in, come among us.[2]

Chapter Twenty

To Mary

Jesus not only brought joy to Joseph, he brought joy to Mary too. In fact, more than anyone else who has ever lived, Mary could have sung with gusto that chorus many of us clamoured to sing in Sunday School:

Joy, joy, my heart is full of joy
Joy, joy my heart is full of joy
My Saviour dear is ever near
That's the reason why my heart
Is full of joy.

In his powerful book *Godzone*, Michael Riddell defines joy with unforgettable freshness:

Joy . . . is when your heart picks up the vibrations of God, and for a brief period of time, beats in harmony; when your love echoes God's love; when your gift resonates with God's. There are moments when you see the funny side of life through God's eyes, and then you just laugh and laugh . . . At other times it's just a deep warm glow; a long slow lingering orgasm of wellbeing. It floods up through you like a warm delicious flush. It makes your eyes shine. In fact you can pick out people in a state of joy, because even if they are crippled with arthritis, their eyes glisten like jewels. Joy is a state of intense aliveness. The more your heart melts with God's, the more often joy erupts.[1]

Writing in a different vein, someone has described joy as 'a delight of the mind'. 'When moderate it is called gladness; raised suddenly to the highest degree it is exultation or transport; when the desires are limited by our possessions it is contentment; high desires accomplished bring satisfaction.'[2]

When I picture Mary listening to Elizabeth's warm and loving welcome, I see a young girl with eyes glistening like jewels singing a song of exultation and leaping and spinning round in a dance of pure, uninhibited delight. When I see her waiting and wondering whether or not Joseph will divorce her, I see her rooted in the realisation that the baby now moving unmistakably in her womb is God's baby – a realisation that sends a surge of joy through the fears and doubts and uncertainties of those dark weeks of her pregnancy. And, having lived in the Middle East and seen for myself how many village people in that part of the world think of the family donkey as a trusted part of the family and a preferred mode of transport to the car, I see Mary riding side-saddle from Naza-reth to Bethlehem, not full of complaints but, rather, content to be carried by this animal who knows her so well, content to be in the company of her sensitive, devoted partner, Joseph, content in the assurance that she and God's baby are safe in the hands of the baby's real Father – Creator God. Had the foetus' Father not worked miracles in Joseph's mind, convincing him that Mary had not been unfaithful to him but faithful to God? Had she not discovered throughout her pregnancy that, wherever she went – to the bazaar or the well, to the fields or to friends, God travelled with her or, more accurately, God travelled *in* her?

Since Jesus brought so much joy to Mary during the fraught days of her pregnancy, how much more must 'a deep warm glow; a long, slow lingering orgasm of wellbeing'[3] have flooded her when she held her baby in her arms, gazed on him with a long, lingering look of love and felt him guzzling at her breasts. Mary, more than any other human being that has ever lived, had entered Godzone – that space that quite literally was inhabited by God. Mary's heart must have frequently picked up the vibrations of God and beat in harmony with those vibrations. Mary's love echoed God's love. Her gift resonated with his and, yes, as she watched her pet donkey and the cows whose steamy breath warmed the air around the manger peer at God's child, she must surely, at times, have seen the funny side of the story? Like any other mother, would she not have chuckled with the baby's heavenly Father as well as with his earthly surrogate father?

At that time the Roman emperor, Augustus, decreed that a census should be taken throughout the Roman Empire . . . All returned to their own towns to register for this census. And because Jospeh was a descendant of King David, he had to go to Bethlehem in Judaea, David's ancient home. He traveled there from the village of Nazareth in Galilee. He took with him Mary . . . who was obviously pregnant by this time.

And while they were there, the time came for her baby to be born. She gave birth to her first child, a son. She wrapped him snugly in strips of cloth and laid him in a manger . . .

(Lk 2:1; 3–7 NLT)

A Response

As you reflect on the joy that Jesus brought to Mary, think back over your own life to occasions when Jesus has brought joy to you. Have there been times, for example, when your eyes have glistened with joy? Re-live them for a while. Enjoy them all over again.

Have there been times when, although things were tough, you have been content? What was happening in your life at the time? Recall the contentment that is a subdued expression of joy.

Have there been days when, like Mary, you have almost gone over the top with joy? What was happening then?

If you have the *Joy to the World* CD or cassette, listen now to the song: *Jesus is our joy.* If you do not have access to the music, read the words, ponder them and ask yourself whether they ring true in your own experience:

> Lovely in your littleness,
> Longing for our lowliness,
> Longing for our lowliness,
> Searching for our meekness.
>
> *Jesus is our joy*
> *Jesus is our joy.*
>
> Peace within our powerlessness,
> Hope within our helplessness,
> Hope within our helplessness,
> Love within our loneliness.
> Held in Mary's tenderness,
> Tiny hands are raised to bless,

Tiny hands are raised to bless,
Touching us with God's caress.

Joy then in God's graciousness,
Peace comes with gentleness,
Peace comes with gentleness,
Filling hearts with gladness.

Jesus is our joy
Jesus is our joy.[4]

A Prayer

My eyes, my eyes
have seen the King.
The vision of His beauty
has pierced me deep within.
To whom else can I go?

My heart, my heart
desires Him.
He's touched something inside of me
that's now reaching out for Him
And I know that I must go.
My God is my love,
my guard, my healing one . . .
my sweet love is Christ,
his heart is my delight,
all my love are You,
O King of Glory.[5]

Chapter Twenty One

To Bethlehem

In his powerful TV documentary, *Son of God*, Jeremy Bowen put a cat amongst some theological pigeons by questioning whether Jesus was actually born in a stable behind a village inn. He posited an alternative theory that has been accepted by many Christians in the Middle East but that often perplexes Christians in the West. The theory is that when Mary and Joseph arrived in Bethlehem, they were not among strangers; rather, because Joseph was 'of the house and line of David' (Lk 2:4–7) they were surrounded by relatives. Many of these would have been distant relatives, but members of the famous family of David nevertheless.

For reasons that I have spelled out in the Appendix to this book, it seems inconceivable that *none* of these relatives provided accommodation for members of their own family. In all probability, then, Mary and Joseph did *not* arrive in Bethlehem while Mary was in labour. Doesn't Luke tell us that it was '*while they were there*' that Jesus was born (Lk 2:6)? Neither did they arrive late at night to be cold-shouldered by an inhospitable inn-keeper who was so heartless that he refused to find them a space in his over-crowded inn. In all probability, Jesus was not born in a stable at all. Rather, he was probably born in a typical, first-century Palestinian home.

Such homes can still be seen near Bethlehem today. In fact, Jeremy Bowen showed us some in the documentary. They have just one living room where the family eat and sleep. On a lower level than this living room is a cave-like space where the family's animals sleep at night. Connecting the family room with the animals' quarters was a row of mangers from which the hungry animals fed. Above the living room was a guest room – rather like the 'prophet's chamber' or 'upper room' where Elijah stayed in the home of the widow of Zarephath (see 1 Kings 17:19,23) or like the 'upper room' where Jesus and his disciples celebrated the Last Supper.

The reason why, for centuries, Christians believed that Joseph and the very pregnant Mary were billeted in a stable behind a Bethlehem inn is that, in *Western* translations of Luke's Gospel, we read that Mary 'laid [Jesus] in a manger because there was no room for them in "the inn".' The Greek word that is translated 'inn' is *katalouma* that simply means a 'room'. Luke uses the same word to describe 'the upper room' where Jesus and his disciples celebrated the Last Supper. Interestingly, Luke does *not* use this word when he relates how the Good Samaritan took the dying Jew to 'an inn'.

If this theory is accurate and, for reasons that I have spelled out in the Appendix, I personally believe that it is, imagine the joy of the relatives of Joseph in whose house Jesus was born. Joseph's relatives would be well-versed in the prophecies concerning the Messiah – like this one from Micah:

'But you, Bethlehem Ephrathah,
     though you are small among the clans of Judah,
out of you will come for me
     one who will be ruler over Israel,
whose origins are from of old,
  from ancient times.'

Therefore Israel will be abandoned
     until the time when she who is in
          labour gives birth
and the rest of his brothers return
     to join the Israelites.

He will stand and shepherd his flock
     in the strength of the LORD,
          in the majesty of the name of the LORD his God.
And they will live securely, for then his greatness
     will reach to the ends of the earth.
     And he will be their peace.

(Micah 5:2–5 NIV)

Joseph's relatives, together with the rest of Bethlehem, would have been hanging on to these verses since they were children. In them lay the hope of their salvation from the tyranny of foreign rule. In them, they heard the prophet promise that although their town was, indeed, 'the little town of Bethlehem', one day it was to become great. Its greatness would lie in the birth of the long-awaited Messiah. He, the hope of the salvation of the world, was to be born in David's town – their town. Until he came, they would experience the long labour pains of trouble and tribulation. When the virgin conceived, however, he would come and offer them deliverance from the turmoil that had torn them apart. When he came, he would be no ordinary mortal. His origins pre-dated his conception, stemming from eternity itself. As Jesus himself was to express this mystery: *'Before*

Abraham was I am' (Jn 8:58). When the government lay on his shoulders, his people would be happy. With him as their shepherd, Jews and Gentiles alike would revere their universal King. He would bring peace – the peace within himself would bring peace to his people.

These were some of the hopes the people of Bethlehem had harboured for years as they waited and prayed for the advent of their Messiah. And now, here he was – right in the midst of them – lying in a manger. For those who believed, like Joseph and Mary and their relatives, friends and neighbours, their joy knew no bounds. Their cup of joy simply overflowed.

Then there was the midwife. Doubtless, she had delivered dozens of babies in her lifetime so, when Mary went into labour, there would have been a frantic knocking on her door and she would have been ushered into the tiny house where the birth was taking place. As midwives often say to me, 'Every birth is a miracle'. But this birth – the *virgin birth* – was surely a miracle of miracles that caused Mary's midwife to glow with pure pride, inexpressible joy and a question: '*How could it happen but for God?*'

If you live in a small town in the Middle East, you quickly discover that nothing is secret. When someone dies, news spreads through the community with lightning speed and though the funeral takes place only hours after the person has passed away, everyone attends the funeral. Similarly, when a woman gives birth, no one escapes the opportunity to celebrate the arrival into the world of a new little life. News of the baby's arrival cannot be contained because everyone wants everyone else to rejoice with the baby's parents. For this reason, even before the shepherds reached the manger where Jesus lay, it is probable that friends and family had already had a peep at the Christ-child. *After* their departure, because the shepherds were intent on making doubly certain that the baby's arrival should not remain a secret, the whole town would have expressed their jubilation – almost certainly with music and dancing. As Micah foretold, on this first Christmas Day, they had much to celebrate.

A Response

In the passage from Micah we have been reading together, the prophet gives a breathtaking overview of the way God pieces together the jigsaw of history. Jesus, the uncreated Son who existed before time began, enters the womb of Mary, an unmarried teenager who gives birth in Bethlehem, the smallest of towns – and history is made.

How do you feel about a God who had all this planned from the beginning of time? Does it help you to believe that 'God's clocks keep perfect time?' – that God knows what he is doing? If so, how might this affect your view of today's world? How might it affect your prayers for our nation and the world?

Reflect on the fact that, when Jesus was called to leave his Father's side and come to earth, Mary was called to her special ministry of motherhood. What might have happened if Mary had said 'No'? How might others as well as God's plan be affected if you resist his plan for you?

Micah seems to suggest that, just as labour pains precede the birth of a baby, so suffering often precedes growth and joy. How might that insight spur you on to pray for our world, our nation, your church and community – yourself?

For Prayer

Pray the two prayers on the next page slowly and meditatively, making them your own.

O Holy Child of Bethlehem,
Descend to us, we pray;
Cast out our sin, and enter in;
Be born in us to-day.
We hear the Christmas Angels
The great glad tidings tell;
O come to us, abide with us,
Our Lord Emmanuel.

* * *

O Bethlehem,
little,
but now made great
by the Lord.
He has made thee great
who, being great,
was in thee made little.
What city . . .
would not envy thee . . .
the glory of that Crib?[1]

Chapter Twenty Two

To Angels

Has anyone captured the euphoria the angels expressed that first Christmas morning more powerfully than Handel in his great oratorio, *The Messiah*? I think not. Words alone can never capture the pure joy with which the angels filled heaven and earth as they celebrated that unforgettable night – though Eugene Peterson paraphrases the Gospel account memorably:

> *There were sheepherders camping in the neighbourhood. They had set night watches over their sheep. Suddenly, God's angel stood among them and God's glory blazed around them. They were terrified. The angel said, 'Don't be afraid. I'm here to announce a great and joyful event that is meant for everybody, worldwide: A Saviour has just been born in David's town, a Saviour who is Messiah and Master. This is what you're to look for: a baby wrapped in a blanket and lying in a manger.'*
>
> *At once the angel was joined by a huge angelic choir singing God's praises:*

'Glory to God in the heavenly heights,
Peace to all men and women on earth who please him.'
(Lk 2:8–11 The Message)

Walter Wangerin has also captured the mood dramatically and powerfully. Recalling the night of our Saviour's birth, he calls one of the shepherds Simon:

Simon had gone to lie among the sheep for warmth, but he wasn't sleeping. He was gazing thoughtfully upward and enjoying the periodic huffings and sighs of the larger ewes.

All at once the stars began to explode.
Simon leaped to his feet.
The sheep stumbled up, bleating and running back to the stone walls.
The stars – in tens, and then in tens of thousands – were flashing like white fires in the black sky! They began to move. Like burning bees, like a great whirling swarm of bees, the stars were crossing heaven from the east to the west.

Simon stood immobilized. Even the sheep were fixed in attitudes of aweful fear.
Between the glorious motion of heaven and the dark earth below, there now appeared a single, endless pillar of pure white fire.
And the fire spoke, and Simon understood what it said. The fire cried, 'Don't be afraid!'
No, *not* the fire – but a figure within the fire! The brilliant form of a human, smooth and huge and very beautiful, his feet upon the mountains.
An angel of the Lord!
The angel said: 'I bring you good news of great joy which shall come to all the people. For to you is born this night in the city of David a Saviour who is Christ the Lord! And

this will be a sign for you: you will find a baby wrapped in swaddling cloths and lying in a manger.'

Suddenly that swarm of the fiery heavenly host swooped down and filled the lower skies, praising God and singing:

> *Glory to God in the highest!*
> *And on earth peace to the people with whom*
> *he is pleased!*

How long the enormous chorus lasted, Simon did not know. The air itself was the music of these angels. When they withdrew again to heaven, and the night was dark, Simon thought he could hear nothing but what he had heard, *Gloria*, still ringing in his ears; and he thought he was blinded to the common things around him, stone and sheep, his companions and his own hand.

But the older man that had been snoring whispered, 'Simon?' – and Simon heard that very well.

'Simon,' said the shepherd, 'did you see that, too?'

Simon gazed solemnly at his friend and under common starlight nodded.

The third shepherd joined them.

The old man gaped at them both and whispered, 'And did you hear what the angel said to us?'

Simon nodded.

'It was the Lord,' the old man said. 'It was the Lord who made these things known to us.'[1]

A Response

Before you read on, turn back to the picture on page 88. Gaze at the angel and ponder his message. Then be still and worship and adore the God who sent him and the child whose birth he is heralding.

When a baby was born in Palestine at the time when Jesus came to live among us, local musicians would congregate at the house to greet his arrival into the world with simple music. We are not told whether the musicians of Bethlehem serenaded the new-born King. What we are told is that God sent a vast army of his ministering spirits to greet the birth of his one and only Son with paeons of praise and a never-to-be-forgotten fanfare of glory. Join the angels in doing what the carol invites us to do:

> *Come . . . and worship*
> *Worship Christ, the new-born King.*

* * *

If you have the *Joy to the World* CD play the carol *Joy to the World* as you worship the new-born King.

A Prayer

Almighty Father, Son and Holy Spirit,
eternal, ever-blessed, gracious God,
to me, the least of saints, to me allow
that I may keep a door in Paradise;
that I may keep even the smallest door,
the furthest door, the darkest, coldest door,
the door that is least used, the stiffest door,
if so it be but in Thine house, O God
if so it be that I can see Thy Glory,
even afar and hear Thy voice, O God!
and know that I am with Thee –
Thee, O God.[2]

Chapter Twenty Three

To Shepherds

'Let's go!' That's the response the shepherds made to the angel's invitation to visit the new-born Messiah:

> *When the angels had returned to heaven, the shepherds said to each other, 'Come on, let's go to Bethlehem! Let's see this wonderful thing that has happened, which the Lord has told us about.'*
>
> *They ran to the village and found Mary and Joseph. And there was the baby, lying in the manger. Then the shepherds told everyone what had happened and what the angel had said to them about this child. All who heard the shepherds' story were astonished, but Mary quietly treasured these things in her heart and thought about them often. The shepherds went back to their fields and flocks, glorifying and praising God for what the angels had told them, and because they had seen the child, just as the angel had said.*
>
> (Lk 2:15–20 NLT)

Luke's re-telling of this dramatic revelation leaves many questions unanswered – like, how did the shepherds know where to go? The angels had not told them precisely where the manger stood. Undaunted by the lack of travelling instructions, the shepherds searched until they found Joseph and Mary and the new-born baby wrapped in strips of cloth just as other Bethlehem babies were wrapped when they were born.

We are not told what the shepherds did when they saw the baby. Neither are we told how long they stayed. What we are told is that they believed and that joy overflowed from them from the moment they saw him. Joy flows from *us* when we know that we are loved. God's Christmas gift to these shepherds through the angels was just this: the news that, at the beginning of the new era that the Messiah's birth heralded, they were included and not ignored, accepted and not rejected, chosen and not cast aside for being 'unclean'. For shepherds who were criticised by the rabbis for being ceremonially soiled this healing, liberating message gave them a brand new start in life. No wonder they were bursting with joy. Joy flows from us, too, when we know that we have something worthwhile to share with others. No wonder the shepherds gossipped the gospel to all they met. They had seen the promised Messiah with their very own eyes. They wanted everyone to share the good news. Joy is contagious and those who heard their tale revelled in it. No wonder they returned to their fields and their flocks glorifying and praising God.

A Response

Picture the field where the shepherds were caring for their flocks that memorable night. What can you see? What can you hear? What can you sense? Picture the sky exploding with light. Listen to the message of the angels. Let the music made by the massed choirs of heaven thrill you. Then run with the shepherds to Bethlehem. Search for the manger. Meet Joseph and Mary. Take a peep at the baby lying in the manger. Don't hurry away. Linger. Look. Listen. Love. Adore. Let the joy of Jesus flow into you – and overflow from you.

Ask yourself, 'What has made the greatest impact on me as I have re-lived this never-to-be forgotten night?' Tell God about it – by writing in your journal, perhaps, or by welcoming the baby Messiah into your heart afresh.

from Jacob Jordaens (1593-1678)

A Prayer of Adoration

I bow before the Father
Who made me
I bow before the Son
Who saved me
I bow before the Spirit
Who guided me
In love and adoration
I give my lips
I give my heart
I give my mind
I give my strength
I bow and adore thee
Sacred Three
The Ever One
The Trinity.[1]

The Road to Bethlehem

'O tell us please' the Wise Men asked,
'Which is the way to Bethlehem?'
And men have sought it ever since
To find the way to Bethlehem.

Here twinkle all the bright lit shops;
Are they the stars of Bethlehem?
And churches stand with pretty cribs;
Are these the paths to Bethlehem?

Now travel agents sell their flights
That daily land near Bethlehem.
Should we take train and plane and bus
And so will come to Bethlehem?

But some there are that know the way,
The only way to Bethlehem,
And those are they that we should ask
To find the way to Bethlehem.

You need to travel down and down,
Who seek the road to Bethlehem,
Past all the outward worldly ways
That do not lead to Bethlehem.

Down to the deep centre of your hearts,
To find the road to Bethlehem,
Where your own love can welcome Christ,
That is the way to Bethlehem.[2]

Chapter Twenty Four

To Simeon

Certain ceremonies marked the birth of a baby at the time when Jesus was born. One was the ancient ceremony of purification. When a woman had given birth to a boy, she was considered to be unclean for forty days. During this time, she was not allowed to enter the temple or take part in any religious ceremony. At the end of forty days, she was required to bring to the temple as an offering, a lamb and a pigeon. If the purchase of a lamb was beyond her means, she was permitted to bring 'the offering of the poor' instead. This offering consisted of two pigeons. As Luke reminds us, it was the offering of the poor that Mary brought to the temple with her (Lk 2:24).

At this moment in time in Palestine, hopes of the coming of the Messiah ran high. Most people believed that he would come with pomp and ceremony to rescue his people from their oppressors. A few thought differently, however. These were known as 'The Quiet in the Land'. Instead of dreaming of violence and conquests, armies and power, they devoted themselves to a life of prayer and sustained watchfulness. Patiently, they waited for the time when God would send the promised Saviour. Among these praying people was Simeon:

> *Now there was a man named Simeon who lived in Jerusalem. He was a righteous man and very devout. He was filled with the Holy Spirit, and he eagerly expected the Messiah to come and rescue Israel. The Holy Spirit had revealed to him that he would not die until he had seen the Lord's Messiah. That day the Spirit led him to the Temple. So when Mary and Joseph came to present the baby Jesus to the Lord as the law required, Simeon was there. He took the child in his arms and praised God, saying,*

> *'Lord, now I can die in peace!*
> *As you have promised me,*
> *I have seen the Saviour*
> *You have given to all people.*
> *He is a light to reveal God to the nations,*
> *And he is the glory of your people Israel!'*

> (Lk 2:25–32 NLT)

Picture the scene. Over the years Simeon must have watched scores of babies being carried into the temple. He had never met Mary and Joseph before yet such was his openness to the Holy Spirit, that as soon as Mary and Joseph climbed the temple steps, he knew that the child they were clutching was the promised Messiah. Simeon was not only filled with the Spirit and led by the Spirit, he was so inspired by the Spirit to love, to praise and to worship his Saviour that he took the child who was God into his arms and embraced him with the greatest affection and joy imaginable. 'He held him close to his heart which was as full of joy as it could hold.'[1]

Those moments of intimacy with his Saviour gave birth to the fullness of joy the psalmist describes when he writes: '*You will fill me with joy in your presence*' (Ps 16:11 NIV). It also gave rise to concern for the child's earthly parents. As we have seen in earlier meditations, joy overflows from us when we have something of value to share with others. Simeon had a blessing to pray over Joseph and Mary. He also had a warning to give the mother of the Lord. On the one hand her precious baby would become the greatest joy for countless people. On the other hand he would be rejected and, at times, it would feel as though a sword would pierce Mary's own soul. Yes. Simeon had much to share and, as his joy spilled out of him, he provided Mary with much-needed pastoral care.

There were many reasons why Simeon's cup of joy overflowed that day. Having been promised by God that he would not die until he had seen the Messiah, he waited and waited and waited – year in, year out. Now, at last, the long wait was over and his patience had been rewarded. Doubtless, during these decades of watching and waiting, like many other devout Jews, he poured out his heart in prayer as he looked for signs of the advent of the Messiah. Now he held in his arms the answer to those fervent prayers. Another reason why his cup of joy overflowed that day was because the ancient prophecies that foretold the coming of the Messiah and filled his people with hope century after century had been fulfilled in the person of the child who gazed into his face this very moment.

In Simeon we witness someone who seemed saturated with the Holy Spirit. The Spirit was on him, spoke clearly to him, praised God, prophesied, loved and blessed others through him. Paul reminds us that the fruit of the Spirit is joy – a fruit that Simeon bore in abundance.

Such joy has to find an outlet. Simeon's joy expressed itself in a stream of affirmation, encouragement, praise and blessing. He praised God for keeping his promise. He affirmed and encouraged both Jews and Gentiles alike prophesying that the whole world would be blessed by the birth of the baby in his arms. He so ministered to Mary and Joseph, prophesying that

Jesus would be the greatest joy of many people that 'they were amazed at what was being said about Jesus' (Lk 2:33 NLT). And he so cared for the pain that Mary, in particular, would have to face as this child's mother that, gently, he warned her that the going would not always be easy.

A Response

Joseph and Mary marvelled at the welcome the old man Simeon gave to Jesus. Do you similarly warm to him? If so, what is it that draws you? If not, do you know why?

On seeing Jesus, Simeon took him in his arms. How do you sense he felt as he held his Messiah so close to his heart? If you had been there, how might you have felt? What might you have done? We cannot hold the Christ-child in our arms but we have him as the indwelling One. What kind of response does that draw from you?

Simeon seems to have been a great encourager. To encourage means 'to pour courage in'. Who might you be able to encourage today?

Simeon was inspired, overshadowed, influenced, directed and protected by the power of the Holy Sprit. What part does the Holy Spirit play in your life?

Write your own prayer as you reflect on Simeon's life and testimony and ministry.

For Prayer

Lord God,
I desire to be like Simeon –
so still before you
that I can hear
and respond to
every prompting of your Spirit,
so in tune with you
that I may become
a sensitive, loving mouthpiece
for you,
so grafted into you
that I may bear your fruit:
love, joy, peace,
patience, kindness, goodness,
faithfulness, gentleness and self-control.
As this New Year unfolds,
give me the quiet trust
that watches
and waits,
that listens
and believes
in you
at all times
and in all places
and that blesses others.[2]

Chapter Twenty Five

To Anna

An elderly widow rang me up while I was in the middle of writing this book. When I asked her how she was, her response was both genuine and warm:

'I'm really well, dear. And all I can think is that, at my age, since the Lord has given me such good health, he must still have work for me to do!'

As I put the phone down, I thought of Anna – the elderly widow who was in the wings watching while Simeon took Jesus from Mary's arms, held him in his own and expressed his joy so effusively:

Anna, a prophet, was also there in the Temple. She was . . . very old. She was a widow, for her husband had died when they had been married only seven years. She was now eighty-four years old. She never left the Temple but stayed there day and night, worshipping God with fasting and prayer. She came along just as Simeon was talking with Mary and Joseph, and she began praising God. She talked about Jesus to everyone who had been waiting for the promised King to come and deliver Jerusalem.

(Lk 2:36–38 NLT)

Anna's life had not been easy. To have been widowed after only seven years of marriage must have been a bitter blow. As Jocelyn Murray explains in her book *Windows on*

Widowhood, vulnerability of widows in the ancient Middle East was notorious:

> It was a society which depended heavily on human muscle power for subsistence. A family composed of a widow and her children found it difficult to survive. If the widow had no adult male relative to act as her legal protector she was in danger of abuse and exploitation. With no insurance or social welfare system, she was in a precarious position.[1]

As though these problems were not painful enough, the belief that society held about widowhood was that it was a reproach from God causing widows to feel private shame and to suffer public humiliation.

Did Anna's devotion to God pre-date the death of her husband, I wonder? Or did she, like Ruth, discover in the early years of her loss that God's compassion for widows is self-evident? Had he not decreed that no one was 'to take advantage of a widow' (Exod 22:22) but rather, at harvest time, 'grain was to be left in the fields, olives were to be left on the trees and grapes on the vines so that the poor (that included widows) could gather sufficient to eat'.[2]

We are not told when Anna found that God was her refuge and strength. What we are told is that, at some stage, she gravitated towards the Temple in Jerusalem. Some believe that she even set up a humble home in one of the Temple's outbuildings. What we are also told is that, like those who live in some convents and monasteries today, she was caught up in a rhythm of worship and prayer, fasting and waiting that ensured that the mystery of God was never far from her thoughts and prayer became to her like breathing. Here in the Temple, like Simeon, she received her call to wait – and wait and wait for the coming of the Messiah.

Sue Monk Kidd has said:

Waiting provides the time and space necessary for grace to happen . . . When you're waiting, you're not doing nothing. You're doing the most important something there is. You're allowing your soul to grow up. If you can't be still and wait, you can't become what God created you to be.[3]

This unassuming, waiting woman was also a prophetess. Surely, she was also as much inspired and guided by the Holy Spirit as Simeon was? Was it not the Holy Spirit who prompted her to witness that wonderful moment when worship of the infant Jesus flowed from Simeon like water cascades from a waterfall? Prompted by the Spirit, Anna came, Anna saw, Anna heard. Instinctively, Anna knew that she was feasting her eyes on

To Anna, this baby was the pearl of great price

the Child of Promise: the Messiah. To her, this baby was the pearl of great price – more valuable than many, many diamonds. Such was her joy that she could not contain it. Praise and heart-felt thanks poured out of her as well as Simeon.

Joy is contagious and Anna knew that she must share her joy with others. Some commentators believe that, while Simeon and Anna were praising God so unreservedly and exuberantly, the Hour of Prayer was in progress in which case they had an uninvited audience. Luke doesn't tell us the time of the Simeon–Anna duet. What he does emphasise is that Anna's joy spilled over to countless others as she spread the news of the Saviour's birth to all who would listen. Many believe that one way in which she spread the good news was that she personally visited all those who over the years had betrayed the fact that they, too, were yearning for the coming of the true Messiah; that she went from door to door testifying that their prayers had been answered; that the Messiah had arrived.

A Response

Picture this watching, waiting, worshipping woman becoming ever more focused on and beautiful for God. Picture her appearing in the temple while Simeon held the baby Messiah in his arms. Sense the completion of her joy. Picture her going from door to door spreading the stupendous news of the Saviour's birth. Then ask yourself, 'How do I feel about Anna?'

Someone has made this claim: 'We are always wanting to put God on escalators to go the next stage of faith as quickly as possible.'[4] Does that apply to you? If so, what can you learn from Anna?

Think of widows you have known who remind you of Anna. Thank God for them.

If you have the *Joy to the World* CD, listen to the prayer, *One*

Thing I Have Asked of the Lord. If you do not have the CD, pray with the words:

> One thing I have asked of the Lord,
> this is what I seek:
> that I may dwell in the house of the Lord
> all the days of my life;
> to behold the beauty of the Lord
> and to seek Him in His temple.

> Who is it that you seek?
> **We seek the Lord our God.**

> Do you seek Him with all your heart?
> **Amen. Lord, have mercy.**

> Do you seek Him with all your soul?
> **Amen. Lord, have mercy.**

> Do you seek Him with all your mind?
> **Amen. Lord, have mercy.**

> Do you seek Him with all your strength?
> **Amen. Christ, have mercy** [5]

Like Anna

Jesus,
I would worship you as Anna did,
I would live for you as Anna did.
Like her I would
submit my whole being to you,
that my conscience may be quickened by your
holiness,
my mind nourished by your truth,
my imagination purified by your loveliness,
my will surrendered to your purpose,
my heart flooded by your love.
Like Anna,
may my whole being focus on you
in selfless adoration, ceaseless love and constant
praise.[6]

Chapter Twenty Six

To the Magi

'This child shall be a light to lighten the Gentiles.' That's a prophecy Simeon breathed as he held his Saviour in his arms. Did Joseph and Mary discuss the ways in which this prophecy would be fulfilled? Or did they simply watch and wait and pray? We are not told. What we are told is that the prophecy was fulfilled in an unexpected and spectacular way while Jesus was still a child. Matthew relates it like this:

Not long after [Jesus'] birth there arrived from the east a party of astrologers making for Jerusalem and enquiring as they went, 'Where is the child born to be King of the Jews? For we saw his star in the east and we have come here to pay homage to him.'

When King Herod heard about this he was deeply perturbed, as indeed were all the other people living in Jerusalem. So he got all the Jewish scribes and Chief Priests together and asked them where 'Christ' should be born. Their reply was: 'In Bethlehem, in Judaea . . .'

Then Herod summoned the wise men to meet him privately and questioned them closely as to the exact time when the star appeared. Then he sent them off to Bethlehem saying, 'When you get there, search for this little child with the utmost care. And when you have found him come back and tell me – so that I may go and worship him too.'

The wise men listened to the King and then went on

*their way to Bethlehem. And now the star, which they had
seen in the east, went in front of them as they travelled until
at last it shone immediately above the place where the child
lay. The sight of the star filled them with indescribable joy.*

*So they went into the house and saw the little child
with his mother Mary. And they fell on their knees and
worshipped him. Then they opened their treasures and
presented him with gifts – gold, incense and myrrh.*

(Mt 2:1–5; 7–11 JBP)

We are not told where the Magi were when they saw 'the
star'. Some believe they lived in Yemen, others in Oman
where, to this day, frankincense may easily be found. Yet
others believe the Magi travelled from Southern Arabia, while
one tradition insists that they came from Persia. The nature of
'the star' also remains a mystery. Beckoning as it did from the
star-studded clarity of a Middle Eastern sky, many believe it
must have been a meteor; others believe it to have been an
appearance of the Holy Spirit.

What matters more than the nationality of the Magi or the
nature of 'the star' is the attitude of these men who made such
a lengthy, laborious pilgrimage to pay homage to Jesus. Their
determination to reach their destination and their generosity in
choosing such significant gifts for the new-born heavenly King
have much to teach us. The reigning earthly king could do
nothing to dampen their enthusiasm or persuade them to turn
back. Having been beckoned by the star, they pressed on and
on and on. There was to be no turning back until their mission
was completed. Their reward was pure joy. The reason for their
joy was a curious open secret:

*The child that lies in the manger, helpless and abandoned to
the love of His creatures, dependent entirely upon them to be
fed, clothed and sustained, remains the Creator and Ruler of
the universe.*[1]

We may share their joy by similarly feasting our gaze on the Christ-child, remembering who he is, marvelling at the mystery of it all – and worshipping him.

William Temple described worship in this way:

Worship is the submission of all our nature:
a quickening of conscience by his holiness,
a nourishment of mind by his truth,
a purifying of the imagination by his beauty,
the opening of the heart by his love,
the surrender of the will to his purpose.
All this is gathered up in adoration which is the most selfless emotion of which we are capable.[2]

A Response

Spend some time worshipping the Christ-child in the way William Temple describes. Spend time, too, reflecting on the significance of the message of the Magi – that God's love is for Gentiles as well as Jews. In other words, Jesus brings joy to the whole world: men and women, every tribe and race and nation.

> The Child of Glory,
> The Child of Mary,
> laid in a manger,
> the King of all,
> who came to the wilderness
> and in our stead suffered;
> happy are those who are near
> to Him.[3]

A Prayer

Pray this prayer – slowly, meditatively, phrase by phrase:

> Lord Jesus Christ,
> Sun of righteousness
> Shine on us
> Scatter the darkness from our path
> And give us peace
> Joy
> and everlasting life.[4]

* * *

Gaze at today's picture of the Christ-child. If you have the *Joy to the World* CD, listen to the following song, then ponder and, if you can, echo the following Declaration of Faith. If you do not have access to the CD, simply read the words slowly, ponder them and echo them:

> To whom shall we go?
> You have the words of eternal life,
> and we have believed
> and have come to know
> that You are the Holy One of God.

> Praise to You,
> Lord Jesus Christ,
> King of endless glory.[5]

Chapter Twenty Seven

To the World

For weeks, it seems, I have woken up to grey skies and forbidding clouds. This morning, though, the valley below my home is flooded with light. As a result, I sense I catch a glimpse of the *joy* with which Isaiah wrote this prophecy:

The people who walk in darkness will see a great light – a light that will shine on all who live in the land where death casts its shadow. Israel will again be great, and its people will rejoice as people rejoice at harvestime. They will shout with joy like warriors dividing the plunder. For God will break the chains that bind his people and the whip that scourges them . . .

For a child is born to us, a son is given to us. And the government will rest on his shoulders. These will be his royal titles:

Wonderful, Counsellor, Mighty God, Everlasting Father, Prince of Peace.

His ever expanding, peaceful government will never end. He will rule forever with fairness and justice from the throne of his ancestor David. The passionate commitment of the Lord Almighty will guarantee this!

(Is 9:2–4; 6–7 NLT)

John takes up the theme of light in the prologue to his Gospel. Speaking of Jesus, he claims:

Everything was created through him,
    nothing – not one thing! –
came into being without him.
What came into existence was Life,
    and the Life was Light to live by.
The Life-Light blazed out of the darkness;
    the darkness couldn't put it out.

           (Jn 1:3,5 The Message)

The Life-Light that shines out of darkness and into our darkness is Jesus. The 'true light that gives light to everyone' is Jesus. His is the light that no darkness, however menacing, will be able to snuff out; the light that shines on our chaos and creates order and beauty, the light that illuminates our pilgrim path.

As though that good news was not enough, there is more. This light is for *everyone*. God loved *the world* so much that he sent his Son for Jews and non-Jews alike, for men and women alike, for rich and poor alike, for the educated and the illiterate alike. His love never draws boundaries. As he himself expressed it, 'I am the light of the world' (Jn 8:12).

Has anyone portrayed this more powerfully than Calvin Miller in his poetic allegory *The Singer?* Here, Earthmaker (God) and his Troubadour (Jesus) are found sitting on the outer rim of space gazing at the newly-created planet earth. Earthmaker reaches out his hand and holds planet earth to his ear:

'They're crying, Troubadour,'
    he said. 'They cry
So hopelessly.' He gave the
    little ball
Unto His Son, who also held
    it by
His ear. 'Year after weary
    year they all

Keep crying. They seem born to
    weep then die . . .
Then with his nail He scraped
    the atmosphere
And both of them beheld the
    planet bleed.

Earthmaker set earth spinning
    on its way
And said, 'Give Me your vast
    infinity
My Son; I'll wrap it in a bit
    of clay.
Then enter Terra microscopically
To love the little souls who
    weep away
Their lives.' 'I will,' I said,
    'set Terra free.'
And then I fell asleep and all
    awareness fled.
I felt my very being shrinking
    down.
My vastness ebbed away. In dwindling
    dread.
All size decayed. The universe
    around
Drew back. I woke upon a tiny
    bed
Of straw in one of Terra's
    smaller towns.

And now the great reduction has begun:
Earthmaker and His Troubadour are one.[1]

A Response

Read and re-read that quotation from *The Singer* letting your imagination picture the scenes that are painted. Notice what feelings the quotation brings to the surface for you. Tell God about them – perhaps writing to him in your journal.

For the past ten years while I've been working for a missionary society, I've travelled to parts of the world that are teeming with people who have never yet heard that God loves us so much that he gave us his Son. After living overseas and then returning to this country, I realised that you don't have to travel abroad to meet such people. More and more, people in the West live without the awareness that the Light of the World has come to dispel the darkness of sin and uncertainty and lovelessness. Commit yourself to such people today as you echo the following prayer:

> *Only in Him we live,*
> *Our lamp light only His,*
> *Our lives for wick we give;*
> *Lamp, oil, flame*
> *JESUS is.*[2]

There are dark corners in all of us: the darkness of unhealed hurts, the darkness of bitterness, resentment and hatred that has been harboured for years, the darkness of sins committed in the past whose memory lurks like a skeleton in the cupboard of our minds. Ask God to beam the bright rays of his light into the nooks and crannies of your life. When your hurts are healed, your bitterness dropped or your sins forgiven, you, too, will come closer to experiencing joy in all its fullness.

A Prayer

Enfold us in your love, dear God,
Yet pierce our hearts with your mercy.
In the cascading of your compassion
Scour away all that offends.
Wash us thoroughly from our wickedness,
And cleanse us from our sin.
Our failures weigh heavy on our hearts . . .

We were formed in the midst
Of a world gone wrong:
From the moment of our conceiving
We breathed our ancestors' sin.
The truths of our sin are hidden
So deep, so secretly:
Bring the light of your wisdom
To the depths of our hearts . . .
May the piercing light of Christ
Illuminate our hearts and minds,
That we may remember in truth
All our sins and God's unfailing mercy.
For we also remember dear God,
How much you love us and all the world;
You have given yourself to us in Jesus Christ,
That we might not perish
But have abundant life.[3]

A Liturgy

The people who walked in darkness
have seen a great light.
For those who lived in a land of deep shadows —
Light! Sunbursts of light![4]

Alleluia

You'll have no more need of the sun by day
nor the brightness of the moon at night.
God will be your eternal light.[5]

Alleluia

You're a fountain of cascading light,
and you open our eyes to light.[6]

Alleluia.

The Life-Light blazed out of the darkness;
the darkness couldn't put it out.[7]

Alleluia

O Come let us adore him,
Christ the Lord.

Chapter Twenty Eight

To Nazareth

I was travelling in a bus in Cyprus on one occasion when the Cypriot bus driver's face suddenly lit up. We were driving past his village at the time. He pointed to it and explained that one of the villagers had just returned after living in Australia for thirty-seven years. Tears of joy and excitement and glee overflowed from this man who had missed his friend so much. Joy is contagious. It touched and filled me as I listened to the way the villagers were saying 'Welcome' to the returnee – those who were old enough to remember him and those who knew him only by hearsay.

Imagine, then, the welcome Mary, Joseph and Jesus would have received when they returned to their home in Nazareth. Having lived in Bethlehem and Egypt, they must have been sorely missed. How Mary must have been hugged and kissed by her parents on her return as well as by her other relatives and friends. Joseph, too, would have received a rapturous welcome from relatives, friends and neighbours. As I discovered for myself when I lived overseas, in a town where there were no furniture shops, a good carpenter is an important person in the community – one that people like to befriend! And, of course, having heard rumours of his birth being announced by angels, rumours of shepherds and wise men from the East visiting him when he was born, the curiosity level concerning Mary's little boy would have soared sky high. Everyone would be agog to see him for the first time.

Jesus seems to have brought joy to the people of Nazareth right from the start. A throw-away but all-embracing sentence in Luke's Gospel assures us of this. As this verse has been variously translated:

Jesus grew both in height and in wisdom, and he was loved by God and by all who knew him.

(Lk 2:52 NLT)

Jesus matured, growing up in both body and spirit, blessed by both God and people.

(The Message)

As Jesus grew up in body and mind, he grew also in the love of God and of those who knew him.

(JBP)

Jesus increased in wisdom, in stature, and in favour with God and people.

(NJB)

From the many references the adult Jesus made to nature, it may safely be assumed that his love of the countryside stemmed from childhood. Imagine his delight in springtime when the hard, parched earth suddenly became a blaze of colour as early anemones carpeted the ground and blossom smothered the fruit trees. Imagine his delight in summer as the grapes on the vines that climbed the trellises outside the tiny homes ripened and begged to be cut and eaten. Imagine him listening to and imitating the donkey, the sheep, the oxen, the cows and the cockerels: 'Baa!' 'Cock-a-doodle-doo!' 'Moo!' – just like children do today. Imagine him running his fingers over the twisted trunks of the olive trees and helping gather the olive harvest. Imagine him gazing up at the velvet, star-studded night sky when there were no neon lights to blur the beauty. Imagine him tuning into the sounds of the deep stillness of the night. Imagine him drinking in the heady perfume of jasmine or orange blossom that fills the air on balmy evenings.

Just as children love to explore the countryside with its delights, so Middle Eastern villagers whose lifestyle suggests that they have all the time in the world to stand and stare, love to reveal to those who will listen nature's hidden secrets: where the birds nest, where delicious herbs can be picked, where and when migratory birds come and go. No wonder Jesus grew in wisdom. No wonder the villagers loved him.

Jesus was not just a country-lover, though. If he had had the opportunity, he would have been a bookworm. He was not only a child who loved to learn, he was a child who was determined that he would live his life God's way. With a flair for languages (he would have spoken Aramaic and read Hebrew and Greek), he must have been a joy to teach. So he would have found favour with the rabbis.

When he was old enough, he almost certainly served his apprenticeship alongside Joseph in the carpenter's shop and the men in the village would take great delight in calling into the workshop to gossip and to watch and encourage him. Was Jesus' compassion for people born right here where he met rich and poor alike and where he heard many stories about villagers – some sad and some happy.

From Joseph, too, he would have learned to pray the liturgical prayers that were said in the synagogue and from Mary the prayer of stillness that was so important to her. The devout of the village would have discerned the depth of his spirituality and warmed to him. From Mary, too, he would have discovered the delights that he mentions in his similes and parables – the agony of losing something as precious as a coin, the fun of watching a lump of dough rising, the excitement of shopping in the bazaar where sparrows seemed so cheap (Mt 10:29).

Yes, the adult Jesus betrays the wonder and the absorption with God's world that is born in childhood with all its questions and exploration and adventure. As Michel Quoist reminds us, it is not just adults who find themselves drawn to such children. In *Prayers of Life* he has God claiming that he likes young people because of the look in their eyes – that nothing is more beautiful 'than the pure eyes of a child'. No eyes were ever more pure than the sparkling eyes of the Christ-child as he discovered from a new angle the wonders that he, himself, had created. Happiness, like joy, is contagious. Undoubtedly, Jesus spread joy and happiness to those with whom he mixed. Undoubtedly he brought many blessings to Nazareth.

Nothing is more beautiful than the pure eyes of a child

A Response

Think of children you know and love. What is it that endears
them to you? What is it that they give you that makes them so
special? Thank God for them, then reflect on Jesus' claim that
'unless you turn round and become like children, you will
never enter the kingdom of Heaven' (Mt 18:3 NEB). As we have
seen, one of the things that children automatically do is
appreciate the wonders of God's creation with all their senses:
sight and hearing, smell and touch. As you go about your daily
tasks today, imagine that you are a child seeing and hearing and
sensing the things around you for the first time. Find joy in the
colour of a tomato or in the beauty of birdsong or . . . then say
the following prayer:

Joy

As the hand is made for holding
and the eye for seeing,
You have fashioned me, O Lord,
for joy.
Share with me the vision
to find that joy everywhere:
in the wild violet's beauty,
in the lark's melody,
In the face of a compassionate person,
in a child's smile,
in the love of parents,
in the purity of Jesus.[1]

For setting me free
to delight in
donkeys and trees,
sun and moon,
sky and stars,
extravagant colours
and miniature wild flowers,

I praise you, O God.

For begging me to enjoy
the filigree-fragrance of the almond blossom,
the blues and turquoises of the sea,
starlike grasses
and open-faced anemones

I praise you, dear Lord.

For prompting me to chuckle
at the antics of ducks
and monkeys,
of turtles
and striped fish,

I praise you, Creator God.

For the sheer **enjoyment** of your world
I give you thanks.[2]

Joy Produced

Chapter Twenty Nine

Obedience

Will I ever forget the first Christmas our first grand-child spent with us? Ben arrived with his parents on Christmas afternoon. The rest of our family were already with us. That evening, at 7.30 pm, the lights of the Christmas tree twinkled, the candles on the table burned brightly and the aroma of cooked turkey and Christmas pudding wafted from the kitchen to the dining room. With gratitude that, after many Christmasses apart, at last we could be together as a family, we sat round the old oak table – expanded for the occasion – and thanked God for his goodness to us.

Our plates were piled high with turkey and all the trimmings when three-month-old Ben began to cough – and cough and cough. This coughing fit left him gasping for breath and wheezing in an alarming way. Neither the lights on the Christmas tree nor removing him from the room where the air was now acrid with the smell of candle wax succeeded in stopping the cough.

'I think we should call the doctor,' I said to my daughter-in-law. Within minutes, the doctor was with us. As she listened to the baby's chest, she shook her head sadly. 'It's bronchiolitis,' she explained. 'A child's form of bronchial asthma. It's hospital straight away, I'm afraid. I'm so sorry . . .'

My daughter-in-law and I were left speechless. The doctor left and silently and helplessly I watched my son and daughter-in-law hastily wrap Ben in a blanket and drive off into the bleakness of a misty night to find a hospital they had never been to before. As I waved them goodbye, I felt I caught a glimpse of how Mary and Joseph might have felt that night when God spoke to Joseph through a dream:

'Get up. Take the child and his mother and flee to Egypt. Stay until further notice. Herod is on the hunt for this child, and wants to kill him.'

Joseph's response was prompt and unquestioning:

Joseph obeyed. He got up, took the child and his mother under cover of darkness. They were out of town and well on their way by daylight. They lived in Egypt until Herod's death.
(Mt 2:13–15 The Message)

'Joseph obeyed.' There could have been little joy in Joseph's heart that night. Only the kind of terror and panic that creates a pit in your stomach and questions that add wings to your feet: *Can we make it in time? Will Herod's troops track us down and kill our precious charge – and us?*

Joseph's prompt, unquestioning obedience undoubtedly saved Jesus' life that night. As we have already recalled, this was not the first time he had changed his plans in obedience to God's word whispered in a dream. Neither would it be the last. When the time came for the family to leave Egypt, God made this clear to Joseph in yet another dream. And Joseph was not the only one to be spurred into action through a dream at this time. God had also persuaded the Magi to leave Bethlehem and to return home, not via Herod as planned, but to re-route and return a different way. The urgency of this message was delivered in a dream also.

In a dream, they were warned not to report back to Herod. So they worked out another route, left the territory without being seen, and returned to their own country
(Mt 2:12 The Message).

Take the child and his mother and flee . . .

A Response

Andrew Murray once claimed that 'obedience is the one certificate of a Christian character'. Someone else has observed that obedience is the test of whether or not we are in fellowship with God. Joseph and Mary and the Magi gave Jesus 'the gold of obedience' when they fled from Bethlehem. Supposing they had disobeyed. Imagine the outcome. Let it help to remind you of Peter's claim that we are created to be 'obedient children' (1 Pet 1:14) – those who carry out the will and Word of God. For most of us, obedience neither comes naturally nor easily. The key, according to Jesus, is love:

> *The person who knows my commandments and keeps them, that's who loves me.*

> (Jn 14:15,21 The Message)

Prayers

Ask for God's grace to go where he leads and to do as he asks today and always:

Ask, too, for the willingness, like Joseph and the Magi to go where God leads and when:

The road stretches out, and as I take one step,
and two, the road moves on.
No end in sight. Just new horizons.
But you are there, taking the steps as I take them.
Sharing the adventure.

Lord, it's risky. There's so much space.
But the real shelter is not in the walls I build.
It's in you.[2]

You prompted the Magi
to abandon their own plans, Lord,
to return to their homes
via a different route.
I, too, have known that prompting
and you implanted in me the willingness
to abandon my own well-laid plans for yours.
Beckon me afresh
and though I may see no reassuring guiding star,
make unmistakably plain
the path you would have me tread.[1]

Praise God for who he is and ask that you may worship him in your life with the gold of obedience.

Hold into God's love and care today all who are anxious about their loved ones and all who nurse sick children. Pray, too, for doctors and nurses on duty this Christmastime.

O Brother Jesus, who as a child was
carried into exile,
Remember all those who are deprived of their
home and country,
Who groan under the burden of anguish
and sorrow,
Enduring the burning heat of the sun,
The freezing cold of the sea, or the humid heat
of the forest,
Searching for a place of refuge.
Cause these storms to cease, O Christ.
Move the hearts of those in power
That they may respect the men and women
Whom you have created in your own image;
That the grief of refugees may be turned
into joy,
As when you led Moses and your people
out of captivity.[3]

Chapter Thirty

Gifts

'There really was a man named Jesus!' That's the way British TV presenter Jeremy Bowen started the first of three programmes simply entitled *Son of God*. 'And there could well have been a bright morning star,' he continued with undeniable excitement. Jeremy Bowen went on to explain that research has revealed that, in the year Jesus was born, the appearance of the planet Jupiter would have seemed like a gigantic star that was visible by day as well as by night. He also suggested that these visitors 'from the East' were almost certainly astrologers. Spotting this spectacular 'star' and sensing that it heralded the birth of a king, they set out on a pilgrimage that had only one aim: to pay homage to the baby.

> *After Jesus was born in Bethlehem village, Judah territory – this was during Herod's kingship – a band of scholars arrived in Jerusalem from the East. They asked around, 'Where can we find and pay homage to the newborn King of the Jews? We observed a star in the eastern sky that signaled his birth. We're on pilgrimage to worship him.'*
>
> *When word of their inquiry got to Herod, he was terrified – and not Herod alone, but most of Jerusalem as well. Herod lost no time. He gathered all the high priests and religion scholars in the city together and asked, 'Where is the Messiah supposed to be born?'*
>
> *They told him, 'Bethlehem, Judah territory. The*

prophet Micah wrote it plainly . . .'

Herod then arranged a secret meeting with the scholars from the East. Pretending to be as devout as they were, he got them to tell him exactly when the birth-announcement star appeared. Then he told them the prophecy about Bethlehem, and said, 'Go find this child. Leave no stone unturned. As soon as you find him, send word and I'll join you at once in your worship.'

Instructed by the king, they set off. Then the star appeared again, the same star they had seen in the eastern skies. It led them on until it hovered over the place of the child. They could hardly contain themselves: They were in the right place! They had arrived at the right time!

They entered the house and saw the child in the arms of Mary, his mother. Overcome, they kneeled and worshiped him. Then they opened their luggage and presented gifts: gold, frankincense, myrrh.

(Mt 2:1–5,7,8 The Message)

Much has been made of these gifts over the years. The Jewish theologian Alfred Edersheim believes that they were symbolic. Gold, a gift fit for a king, marked Jesus' royal status and underlined the high regard in which the royal baby was held by these visitors from the East. Myrrh, because it was used to embalm the body in preparation for burial, was considered to be an emblem of Jesus' humanity that foreshadowed his all-too-early burial. Incense, Edersheim claimed, underlined Jesus' divinity.[1]

Others believe, though, that the gifts brought by the visitors from the East were simply intended as souvenirs from their own country – presents that marked the esteem in which their country held the new-born King. Jeremy Bowen offers yet another theory – that the astrologers' gifts came, not from their homeland, but from a bazaar in Petra, Jordan where they stopped to do some shopping! Here in this major trading centre gold could be bought comparatively cheaply. Here, as in every other bazaar in the Middle East, the scent of frankincense being burned would have filled the air. Here little lumps of myrrh were easy to come across.

Whether Jesus' would-be visitors purchased their gifts in the homeland or in Jordan matters little. What matters more is the ring of authenticity that sounds for anyone who has lived in or visited the countries in question. Even as I write, I recall my own trips to this part of the world and, in my mind's eye, I can see how stunning the women look in their gold jewellery and the enjoyment they have in whiling away time in the jewellers' part of the bazaar. As I picture these women and re-visit in my imagination the colourful bazaars, the sweet scent of the perfume with which the air is filled as stall-holders burn little lumps of frankincense on briquettes of charcoal almost fills my study.

At the same time, I can see the gnarled hands of stall holders holding out greyish lumps of the myrrh they seem so proud of and are keen to sell. 'Eat it!' one such stall-holder said to me as he sold me some. 'Eat it when you have stomach-ache!'

Whether Jesus' impressive visitors did their shopping at home or at a bazaar en route matters little. As Edersheim rightly underlines, what matters most is their generosity and devotion. These, he underlines, are best remembered by silently joining in the homage these wise men from the East paid to the Saviour of the world.

A Response

Thumb through this book until you find a picture of Jesus that draws you to itself for some reason. Spend time gazing at it. Let God speak to you through it. Then ask yourself the question we sing so often at this time of year:

What can I give him, poor as I am,
If I were a shepherd, I would bring a lamb,
If I were a wise man, I would do my part,
Yet what I can I give him,
Give my heart.[2]

Or, if you have the *Joy to the World* CD, listen to the following song:

What can I give to the King?
Give to the One who has everything?
What can I give?
What gift can I bring?
What can I give to the King?
What can I give to the King?
Give him a heart that's opened up wide.
Give him a life that's got nothing to hide.
Give him a heart that's tender and true
And he'll give it all back to you
Yes, he'll give it all back to you.[3]

A Prayer

O God, the source of all insight,
whose coming was revealed to the nations
not among men of power
but on a woman's lap:
give us grace to seek you
where you may be found,
that the wisdom of this world may be humbled
and discover your unexpected joy,
through Jesus Christ,
Amen.[4]

Chapter Thirty One

Hatred

Last year, January 6th dawned bright and with a sunrise that streaked the sky with swirls of pink and purple and gold. January 6th is the day when many Christians celebrate the Feast of the Epiphany – the moment the Magi eventually reached Jesus in Bethlehem. I was on retreat at the time. Just before lunch, the clear blue sky, the sparkling air and the spring-like sunshine tempted me to take a walk around the garden of the convent where I was staying. As I walked, I sang: 'What can I give to the King . . . ?'

As I sang, I became aware of a blackbird and thrush singing full throttle too. A squirrel then scampered across the lawn in front of me and I stumbled over some early daffodil spears that were pushing their noses above ground. My heart and nature seemed full of joy – until I came across a heap of white feathers and a skeleton leaf. The feathers spoke volumes: there had been an altercation between a bird and its predator – a scuffle that had resulted in the death of the bird. The skeleton leaf reminded me of a baby I loved who had died not many months before. The air still sparkled, the birds still sang, the beauty still surrounded me but I had been brought up with a jolt at the reminder that grief and glory so often go together.

Simeon reminded Mary of that reality when he warned her that the arrival of Jesus into the world would bring heartache as well as joy. People would have to make up their minds about him. Some would respond to him with dedicated and adoring love. Others would hate and reject him.

Mary did not have long to wait before this prophecy became a nightmarish reality. Matthew describes how Jesus' existence posed a threat for the ruthless King Herod – how Herod's fear of being usurped triggered off brutality and violence of the cruelest kind – in the mass murder of innocent children:

Herod, when he realized that the scholars had tricked him, flew into a rage. He commanded the murder of every little boy two years old and under who lived in Bethlehem and its surrounding hills . . .

(Mt 2:16–18 The Message)

Any kind of cruelty to children causes an outcry: sexual abuse, bullying, murder, malnutrition, homelessness, child prostitution. This is not the only reason why Matthew's account of 'the slaughter of the innocents' in Bethlehem prompts the question: 'Why?' 'Why did it have to happen?' 'Why, when God seemed to have orchestrated the drama of Jesus' birth so magnificently did he allow this mass murder to take place?' 'Why did he save his Son but fail to protect the twenty or so Bethlehem babies?'

Sadly and frustratingly, there are no answers to these questions – except, 'We are not told.' Perhaps a more helpful approach to the problem is to project ourselves into the little town of Bethlehem as it would have been at the time of the tragedy.

Anyone who has lived in the Middle East will testify to the strength of the bonding that exists between people who live in the same town or village. It is so strong that, if only one baby had been murdered that day, the whole town would have attended the funeral. As we have seen on our television screens in recent years, funerals in this part of the world are not quiet, private affairs. Everyone comes. Everyone weeps openly and loudly – men as well as women. Imagine, then, this tiny town suddenly devastated, not with the death of *one* baby but of *twenty* or more.

Imagine the scene when, because of the heat, twenty or more little bodies must be buried as soon after the murder as possible.

Imagine the grief, the pain, the questions, the cloud that would have descended on that town and that would hover over it for years. Then ask a question that points to a place where the pain of grief and loss and loneliness and rejection may be taken: *'Where is God when it hurts?'* Jesus gives us an answer to this question by reminding us that when a sparrow dies the kind of death the bird in the convent garden died, God knows and God cares. Jesus reminds us that every person on this earth is worth much, much more than many sparrows. How much more, then, did God care about those babies that Herod had butchered to death. How much more does he care as he watches us weep and sees how our hearts are breaking and our spirits bleeding. Sue Ashdown's poem sums up the situation so well:

He Knows

A leaf falls to the ground:
a tiny flutter,
no sound.
He knows.

A sparrow sheds a feather:
the slightest movement,
no noise.
He knows.

A lily bends and breaks in the wind:
no scream of pain;
just silence.
He knows.

A heart lifted in joy:
but whom to tell,
just a smile.
He knows.

A mind torn with pain:
only silence is heard,
no heart's cry.
He knows.

A hand lifted in defence:
no justice felt,
just vulnerability.
He knows.

A soul seeking to follow:
no perfection here,
just sin.
He knows.

A life longing to serve:
no unhindered walk,
but stumbling.
He knows.

A breath drawn in waiting:
no certainty for ease,
just obedience.
He knows.

A whisper from heart's depths:
no eloquent phrases,
just 'My Lord'
He knows,
He knows.[1]

* * *

A Response

It's easy to point the finger at Herod and to feel scandalised at his brutality but, as has often been pointed out, when we point the finger at someone else, three of our fingers point back at us. So we need to ask ourselves: Have I ever felt threatened by anyone – at school, at work, in the community? If so, how did I behave towards them: ostracise them, criticise them, hate them, ignore them, try to put them down? Talk to God about any hurt or hatred, anger or bitterness that you may have bottled up. Then, if you can, either now or over a period of time, open the hurt to God so that he can pour his healing love into it and assure you of his unfailing love. When the hurts have been healed you will be in a better position to let go of any hatred or bitterness or resentment that you have been harbouring and to feel the forgiveness that God longs to give you.

As far as you are able, ask God to remove all hatred from your heart and to replace it with love. If you have the *Joy to the World* CD listen to the Peace Prayer.

Now put the butchering of the babies in its historical context. The tragedy reminds us that it was a brutal world into which Jesus was born. The gruesome, gory story of soldiers marching into a village to slaughter all its babies was only one manifestation of this sad fact. Since then, history has repeated itself over and over again. We have only to switch on our television set, listen to the radio or read a newspaper to be reminded of that sad fact. As now, so then. Joy in some gives birth to jealousy, rivalry, revenge-seeking, hatred, crime in others. The root cause of the problem is sin. Although Jesus was protected on this occasion, the day would come when he would be the victim – when he would complete the journey that started in the cradle but took him to the cross.

Today, as you pray, hold into God's protective love children who are in any kind of danger and parents who, at this time of year, are hurting because of the crimes that have been committed against their babies, toddlers or teenagers. Thank God for sending Jesus to deal with the root cause of cruelty to children – human sin. Ask for the grace to live *your* life as God would have you live it.

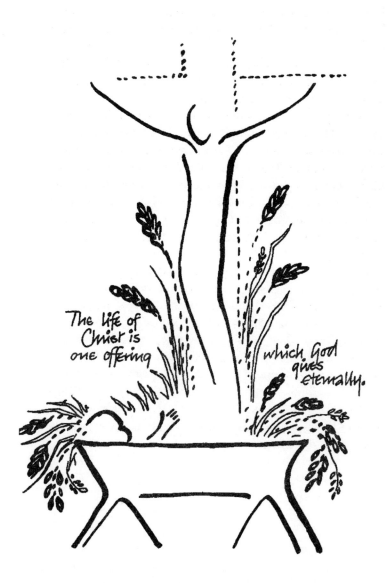

The life of Christ is one offering which God gives eternally.

From the Cradle to the Cross

Chapter Thirty Two

Contemplation and Dedication

The mothers of the massacred babies continued to nurse their grief. The Magi continued their journey home. Simeon and Anna remained in the temple contemplating the mysteries they had witnessed and gossipping the gospel to anyone who had ears to hear. Meanwhile, as we have seen, Mary and Joseph eventually returned to their home in Nazareth. There, for thirty years, Jesus lived, learned, played, grew, matured and was blessed both by God and those who knew him.

Apart from a reference to him travelling to Jerusalem with Jesus and Mary when Jesus was twelve years old, nothing more is heard of Joseph. Tradition insists that he died an early death leaving Mary to bring up Jesus alone. We are told little of Mary during these 'hidden years'. The one thing we are told, though, is that she treasured and pondered the mysteries that had changed the direction of her life: the mystery of Jesus' strange conception and all that had stemmed from it. Luke puts it in a nutshell when he writes:

'. . . *his mother stored all these things in her heart*'
(Lk 2:51 NLT).

His mother held these things dearly, deep within herself.
(The Message)

. . . his mother treasured all these things in her heart'.

(JBP and NIV)

To 'treasure', to 'store things in your heart', to 'keep things dear and deep within yourself' is to contemplate. To contemplate in the middle of 'the muchness and manyness'[1] of travelling or in the middle of the disruption that a transition from one location to another creates or, worse, while you work your way through a bereavement is never easy. Yet Mary seems to have managed it. She models to us the ideal of being active in contemplation and contemplative in action – a form of spirituality that many of us covet.

In some ways, of course, it was easy for Mary to contemplate. Christian contemplation has been described as the prayer of loving attentiveness – paying 'rapt and loving attention to God and to his world'.[2] It involves knowing and loving God in the depths of our being and growing in that love. When we contemplate, our whole being revolves around God rather than around self. When we contemplate, we so place ourselves into the hands of God that he can transform the way we think, the way we feel, the way we behave. When we contemplate, we gaze on God, delight in him and are content to 'just be' with him.

One of the best-loved stories used to describe the prayer of contemplation is that of the old peasant who, after working all day in the fields, would return home via the village church. At the door, he would lay down his pick-axe and spade and wander into the church where he would linger for an hour. The priest of the village would often watch him come and go, wondering precisely why the old man should visit the church with the regularity of clockwork. One day, he could contain his curiosity no longer so, as the peasant prepared to leave, the priest asked him outright: 'Tell me, why do you come into my church every day and just sit there doing nothing?' The peasant looked the priest in the eye and simply said, '*I look at him and he looks at me and we tell each other that we love each other.'* The peasant had discovered what many of us long for and need: the prayer of contemplation.

As Mary held Jesus to her breast or gazed at him in her arms, she was engaging in contemplative prayer. She had the unsurpassable joy of gazing at God incarnate and of knowing that he gazed at her; the unforgettable joy of knowing that, without using any words at all, they were communicating to one another that they loved each other.

That is not to say that Mary spent all day and every day sitting and holding and contemplating the Christ-child. Like any mother, she now faced the challenge of discovering 'The Spirituality of the Family'. In his book *Finding God in the Home,* Ernest Boyer helpfully compares and contrasts Mary's call to that of the disciples:

> *The disciples were called to follow Jesus, Mary and Joseph*
> *were called to feed him; the disciples were called to learn*
> *from Jesus, Mary and Joseph to teach him to speak; the*
> *disciples to stand beside him, Mary and Joseph to help him*
> *to stand. The disciples were called to suffer with Jesus the*
> *pain of his death so that he might give the gift of life. Mary*
> *and Joseph were called to suffer for him the pain of birth so*
> *that he might give the gift of love . . . Through their*
> *relationship with this child their relationship with God*
> *would deepen profoundly.*[3]

Yes, as well as spending time gazing at the God-child, like any mother, Mary dedicated her entire life to serving him: feeding him and playing with him, teaching him to walk and to talk, washing his clothes as well as teaching him to play and to pray. Her days were full and there would have been times when her nights were broken with all that that involves in terms of loss of energy, rise of stress levels, deep-down weariness. Even so, throughout Jesus' life, we see Mary's contemplation of him giving rise to self-dedication: the dedication that searched frantically for him when she imagined he was lost somewhere between Jerusalem and Nazareth (Lk 2:46), the dedication that prompted her to take him on one side during the wedding in Cana and to whisper, 'They have no wine' (Jn 2:1ff), the devotion that drove her from Nazareth to Galilee when she heard that Jesus was so thronged by people that he had no time to eat (Lk 8:19). In each of these instances, Mary was acting as any Middle Eastern mother would have acted towards her unmarried son – offering the kind of mothering that appears to many Westerners like smothering, attempting to ensure that he was unafraid to use his supernatural gifts, attempting to protect him from burn out. Such was her dedication that we find her continuing to contemplate her much-loved Son in that most painful place of all – at the foot of the cross and, without doubt, if there had

been anything practical she could have done to alleviate his
agony that day, she would have done it.

A Response

Whether we are single or whether we are married and whether
or not we have children or grandchildren, the call comes to us
all to ensure that our life revolves around God. The words of a
prayer attributed to St Ignatius sums this up well:

Turn my whole being to your praise and glory.

Ernest Boyer suggests some ways of doing this:

*God is always present to us. The greatest thing we can do in
life is to teach ourselves to be always present to God. The
small, routine tasks that fill every day spent in the care of
others may seem to be a barrier to this, but they need not.
They may in fact be turned into one of the finest spiritual
disciplines, a special sacrament of the routine through which
what to others appears the most ordinary of mundane of tasks
is revealed to be a sacred act, an act of prayer. Prayer is
nothing more or less than this, being present to God. And so
this is a spirituality that makes all of life into prayer, a
prayer of love, a prayer of help for others, a prayer of courage.
It is a prayer that spans a lifetime, a prayer of great beauty.*[4]

He goes on to suggest three ways in which we can incor-
porate this dimension of prayer into our lives: practise the 'prayer
of quiet', 'the prayer of work' and 'the prayer of dialogue'. By this
he means taking at least twenty minutes each day to 'just be' with
God – resting in his love; to whisper a prayer before, during and
after any piece of work or service that we are engaged in, and
spreading before God the breadth and depth of our feelings.[5] In
the coming days practise this prayer for yourself.

Ponder the method of prayer that Mary models: the prayer of contemplation and the prayer of dedication. Which do you sense you need to grow in? Ask God for the grace to develop this area of your life. Ponder the practical suggestions Ernest Boyer makes. If one or more of them beckons you, focus on it, try it and write to God about it. Now pray two of Ernest Boyer's

Two Prayers

Dear God,
Whose name is Love,
who in love and with love formed all that is,
teach me to see the great worth of those small,
everyday tasks involved in the care of others.
Teach me to see them for what they are:
re-enactments of the greatest truth there is,
the truth of your unfailing care for me and for all that is.[5]

* * *

You are with us, Lord,
but how seldom we know it.
Open our eyes,
open our hearts.
teach us to see
and to feel
that we are not alone,
that you are with us
in all we do,
embracing us
with your love
and your care.[6]

Chapter Thirty Three

A Call

The eighth day after a baby boy's birth was a very important one in first-century Palestine. On this day, the child was circumcised. This circumcision ceremony was so sacred that it would take place even if the eighth day happened to fall on the Sabbath – that day when most activities were prohibited. One reason why the ceremony was so sacrosanct was that it was a re-enactment of the awesome commitment God made to Abraham:

'I will keep my promise to you and to your descendants in future generations as an everlasting covenant. I will be your God and the God of your descendants. I will give to you and to your descendants this land in which you are now a foreigner. The whole land of Canaan will belong to your descendants for ever, and I will be their God.'
God said to Abraham, 'You also must agree to keep the covenant with me, both you and your descendants in future generations. You and your descendants must all agree to circumcise every male among you. From now on you must circumcise every baby boy when he is eight days old . . . This will show that there is a covenant between you and me.'

(Gen 17:7–11 NRSV)

Recalling how strangely sick I felt as I held my babies while our doctor stuck his needle in their arms when they were being vaccinated, I often wonder how Mary felt as she held her baby during the circumcision ceremony. Did she feel strangely sick as she watched his flesh being pulled, his foreskin being cut away with a knife and drops of blood being shed? If so, how might she have felt had she known that just three decades later, she would stand at the foot of a cross on which he hung bleeding to death? We are not told. What we are told is that the eighth day of a baby's life was significant for another reason. It was the day when the child was named:

> *When the eighth day arrived, the day of circumcision, the child was named **Jesus**, the name given by the angel before he was conceived.*
>
> (Lk 2:21 The Message)

The name Jesus was a common one among the Jews at this time. The root of the name is the Hebrew word *'yasha'* that conceals a cluster of meanings. One is, 'to bring into a spacious environment'. Another is 'to be at one's ease'. The name also means: 'to be free to develop without hindrance', 'wholeness' and 'The Lord saves'. As the angel explained to Joseph before Jesus' birth:

> *'Joseph, son of David . . . Mary's pregnancy is Spirit-conceived. God's Holy Spirit has made her pregnant. She will bring a son to birth, and when she does, you, Joseph, will name him Jesus – 'God saves' – because he will save his people from their sins.*
>
> (Mt 1:20,21 The Message)

Jesus still offers us each of these gifts: wholeness, spaciousness, freedom, forgiveness, salvation, love. He longs that we should become the people he always intended we should be. He longs to give us the security of his love. He longs to pour that love into those places deep within us where we have never experienced love. As we noted earlier in this book, joy wells up in our hearts when we know we are loved. Instead of making a string of New Year resolutions that we will quickly break, then, perhaps we would be wiser to make only one: to open ourselves afresh this year to the unending, outpoured, saving love of Jesus; to place our hands in his in the way one woman describes so memorably:

> I said to the man who stood at the gate
> of the year:
> 'Give me a light that I may tread safely
> into the unknown.'
> And he replied:
> 'Go out into the darkness
> and put your hand into the hand of God,
> that shall be to you better than light
> and safer than a known way.'[1]

A response

Close your eyes and try to picture first Jesus, the baby, shedding drops of blood at his circumcision, then Jesus the man bleeding while he is being flogged by soldiers; bleeding more as he hangs on a cross. Remind yourself of an awe-filled truth: '*He did it for me.*' Then, if you can, pray the words of the familiar hymn that follows, listening to the hymn if you have the *Joy to the World* CD:

Just as I am without one plea
But that Thy blood was shed for me
And that thou bids't me come to Thee
O Lamb of God, I come,

Just as I am, though tossed about
With many a conflict, many a doubt,
Fightings and fears within, without,
O Lamb of God, I come.

Just as I am poor, wretched, blind;
Sight, riches, healing of the mind,
Yea, all I need, in Thee to find,
O Lamb of God, I come.

Just as I am, Thou wilt receive,
Wilt welcome, pardon, cleanse, relieve,
Because Thy promise I believe,
O Lamb of God I come.

Just as I am, Thy love unknown
Has broken every barrier down;
Now to be Thine, yea, Thine alone,
O Lamb of God, I come.

Just as I am, of that free love
The breadth, length, depth and height to prove,
Here for a season, then above,
O Lamb of God, I come.[2]

When we have tasted afresh the constancy of God's love, we may also hear God's call to follow and serve him. When Jesus called his disciples to follow him, he called them first to be *with* him and only then to serve him. As we have seen in these meditations, Jesus came as a baby to show us that he wanted to be held and handled, loved and cherished. We have also seen that what he most wants to give *us* is love. Each Christmas, the call comes to us afresh to love and be loved, to serve and be served, to follow. So, be still for several minutes. Allow God to love you. Bask in that love. Recognise that the great I AM is with you.

I was regretting the past and fearing
the future.
Suddenly, my Lord was speaking:
My Name is I Am.
He paused. I waited. He continued.
'When you live in the past,
with its mistakes and regrets,
it is hard.
I am not there.
My name is not I was.
When you live in the future,
With its problems and fears,
It is hard.
I am not there.
My name is not I will be.
When you live in this moment,
It is not hard.
I am here.
My name is
I Am.[3]

Chapter Thirty Four

A Challenge

In his gripping re-telling of the Magi's visit to Bethlehem, Paul Flucke introduces a powerful twist to the tale. As well as having the Magi bearing the gifts we read of in the Gospels: gold, frankincense and myrrh, he has the angel Gabriel lurking in the place where the Christ-child lay, poised to put certain questions to the seemingly-impressive visitors:

> *'And who are you?'* Gabriel asks Gaspar, the first of the Magi to enter. *'Have you a gift?'*[1]

> On hearing Gaspar confess that he has brought bars of purest gold, Gabriel insists that, *'Your gift must be the essence of yourself. It must be something precious to your soul.'*[2]

> *'Such have I brought'*, Gaspar confides as, confidently and jubilantly he moves closer and closer to the Christ-child, his parents and the watching animals. Just as Gaspar was about to kneel and lay his gold before the child, though, he stopped and stood erect. 'There in his outstretched hands lay, not gold, but a hammer . . . *'But, but –'*, Gaspar stammered . . . And then softly, from behind him, he heard the voice of Gabriel . . . *'You have brought the essence of yourself . . . What you hold in your hands is the hammer of your greed. You have used it to pound wealth*

from those who labour so that you may live in luxury. . .'[3]

Full of shame, Gaspar admitted the truth and turned towards the door to make a quick exit. But Gabriel blocked his path explaining that first Gaspar must leave his gift with the new-born King. Gaspar protested. Gabriel insisted. Slowly and reluctantly, Gaspar turned back to the Christ-child. Having placed his hammer at the baby's feet, slowly, he rose, turned towards the door, paused to look at his Saviour, then rushed outside. While the waiting world watched, a smile wreathed Gaspar's face and he held his hands high in wonder.

Something similar happened to both Melchior and Balthasar. Gabriel cautioned both of them in the way he had warned Gaspar: *'Your gift must be something precious to your soul'*. As Melchior knelt, awed, at the Christ-child's feet, to his horror, his frankincense turned to vinegar. *'You have brought what you are made of'*, observed Gabriel: *'the bitterness of your heart, the soured wine of a life turned grim with jealousy and hate . . .'*[4].

Silently Melchior sidled towards the door until Gabriel insisted that he should leave his gift. *'How I wish I could!'* Melchior replied. *'How long have I yearned to empty my soul of its bitterness.'*[5]

With Gabriel's encouragement and help, Melchior eventually placed his gift at the Saviour's feet. When he came out of the house where the holy family lived, his eyes shone, his skin was as smooth as a youth's and he found himself gazing on horizons he had never seen before.

If you want to know what happened to Balthasar, the third of the Magi, you must read the story for yourself!

I happened to read it when I was on retreat on one occasion. I had never been to this particular retreat centre before so I gasped when I was shown the chapel and found myself standing in front of a beautiful carving of Mary clutching a very energetic Jesus. That evening, I returned to the chapel alone.

There I knelt gazing and gazing at this Child whose arms were stretched as though to say, *'Hold me. I want to come.'*

I looked from this child to my troubled heart that seemed full of resentment and fear as I remembered a situation that had flared up that week. Eventually, though, my eyes wandered from the lively Christ-Child to the huge Cross that hung from the chapel ceiling. The arms of the figure on the Cross were also opened wide. *'The baby wants to be held,'* I mused. *'The Risen Lord wants to hold me. Before either of these miracles can happen, I must come to him in the way Gabriel insists – bringing what I am made of.'*

After a long struggle, I placed my resentment and fear at the feet of the crucified Jesus. Suddenly, my hands and arms were empty – empty enough to receive and hold and cherish the bouncy baby boy Jesus. At that moment, the Convent cat appeared on the chapel steps and settled itself under the Cross. I chuckled, then knelt in wonder, love and praise. Like Gaspar and Melchior, I had brought what I was made of. Like them, leaving what I was made of with Christ had set me free from myself – *free for him.*

A Response

If you were asked to give God what you are made of today, what would you bring? Bring it now. Lay it at his feet knowing that, however inappropriate it seems to be, he will accept it and, if necessary, set you free from it. Then worship your Lord in those familiar words:

O Come let us adore him,
O come let us adore him,
O come let us adore him,
      Christ the Lord.

For He alone is worthy,
For He alone is worthy,
For He alone is worthy,
      Christ, the Lord.

We'll give Him all the glory,
We'll give Him all the glory,
We'll give Him all the glory,
      Christ the Lord.

For more than a month, we have spent time focusing on the Christ who comes, the Christ who came and the Christ who will come again. The challenge that faces us now, in the words of the Risen, Ascended, Soon-Coming One is this:

'God authorized me to commission you: Go out and train everyone you meet, far and near, in this way of life, marking them by baptism in the threefold name: Father, Son, and Holy Spirit. Then instruct them in the practice of all I have commanded you. I'll be with you as you do this, day after day after day after day, right up to the end of the age.'

(Matthew 28 – 18b–20. The Message)

May we go out and do what one of Jesus' devoted
followers suggests:

Totally
Love Him
Who gave
Himself
Totally
For your Love[6]

Appendix

Born in a Stable?

'What are you hoping for from this retreat?' That's a question I put to a young woman one Christmas Eve. Together with others, she had come to our home in Cyprus for the Christmas Retreat that we led each year.

'What I really want is to come closer to God,' came the heart-warming reply. 'The trouble is that I have real problems with Christmas. I just can't believe the Christmas story.'

I remember asking myself as I listened: 'How can you be a Christian, live in Bethlehem and not believe in the Christmas story?' Intrigued, I asked a few more leading questions in the hope of reaching the root of the problem. The root was soon exposed. 'Living as I have in this part of the world for so many years, I just can't believe that, when Mary and Joseph reached Bethlehem, all of their relatives, however distant, would have refused them hospitality. The culture just doesn't work like that,' she explained with feeling. I understood. Since living in Cyprus and becoming steeped in the culture of the island, I had also wondered why Mary and Joseph would have been trying to book themselves into an inn in an area where clearly they both had relatives. The reason why I was puzzled was that I once asked a middle-aged Cypriot waiter, 'Where do you live?' I knew which town he lived in and was curious to know whether he lived in the hills or by the sea. Instead of answering my question in the way a Westerner would have answered it, though, he replied in the way many people from the Middle

East would answer: 'The name of my village is Dhroushia,' he said. 'All my olive trees are there.' He then went on to tell me about his latest olive crop. As I listened, the basic message was still sinking into my Western brain. 'Home is not where you live today, it is where your olive trees are. Home is where you hail from. Home is where your ancestors are buried.'

As I listened to the retreatant and listened to my own questions also, I decided that, when the retreat began, we would let the group speak into the question that was causing such concern:

'Why do you think Mary and Joseph looked for accommodation in the village inn rather than with their relatives that first Christmas night?'

Everyone in the group had lived and worked in the Middle East for several years and had therefore laid on one side the Western mind-set with which we read the Scriptures in the homeland. Each had been moved by the hospitality that is always lavished on a member of the family who returns to the Middle East no matter how long they have been away from home. Each of us could share memories we had of watching a traveller return home and being welcomed with hugs and tears and flowers and meals and, of course, accommodation for as long as they needed it.

'Then why didn't Joseph and Mary go to *their* relatives?' I persisted.

Each member of the group knew and loved and trusted the then Canon Theologian of Nicosia Cathedral, Canon Kenneth Bailey. 'Let's hear what Ken has to say!' we decided. So we watched a video in which this theologian who lived and worked in the Middle East for forty-five years explains where the source of the confusion lies.

Professor Bailey first went to the Middle East at the age of four. He has a flair for languages so speaks fluently and reads a variety of Middle Eastern languages including Hebrew and Greek, Arabic and Aramaic. Over the years, such is his love for

the Bible and the Middle East that he has studied the way
Middle Eastern scholars have interpreted the Scriptures.

There were smiles all round when we heard the first part of
the video. Ken started where we needed him to start – by
explaining that, if you are a Middle Easterner, when you
return to your village after a period away from home, you are
given a rapturous welcome. Church bells are rung, a party is
thrown and any number of relatives and friends insist on
offering you hospitality.

There were smiles all round, too, when our mentor
reminded us that, because Joseph was 'of the house and line of
David' (Lk 2:4), that is, a descendant of the royal line, he could
go to *any* home in Bethlehem and expect to receive, not just a
warm welcome, but hospitality for as long as he needed it. The
Gospel writers remind us that Mary also had relatives within
comparatively easy reach of Bethlehem. Had she not already
stayed with some of them – namely, Zechariah and Elizabeth?
They knew that her baby was due and would doubtless have
welcomed Mary and Joseph with open arms if no accommodation had been available in Bethlehem.

By this time, we were sitting on the edge of our seats, the
sense of expectation and anticipation high. Ken Bailey was on
our wavelength and we on his. Eagerly, we drank in the insights
he shared next. They made so much sense to us since we could
no longer read the Nativity narrative in the way we had done
when we were steeped in the culture of the West.

Ken pointed us to Luke 2 – to the verse that clearly states,
'*While they were still there*, the time came for the child to be
born.' Luke does not say that Mary went into labour as she was
crossing the threshold into Bethlehem. The implication is that
Mary and Joseph had settled into Bethlehem days or even
weeks *before* the baby was born. As we weighed this claim, a
picture of a typical first-century Palestinian house appeared on
our television screen. The house had one room – just as many
houses in the two-thirds world today have just one simple

room. I have seen them on my travels so the diagram did not seem strange. The door of the house did not open onto this room. The door opened onto a lower level of the house – onto the cave-like place where the family sheep and cow and goat were brought at night. Again, having stayed in houses that have been built in this way, it was not difficult for me to picture the scene. Steps led from this lower level of the open-plan dwelling to the upper level – the room where the family ate and slept and relaxed. On a slope that ran down from the family room to the animals' quarters, we could see that a row of mangers had been dug out of the floor. Since they were on a slope, the animals could easily reach them when they needed food and they could also easily be washed out.

Ken reminded us of the message the angels gave to the shepherds: 'You will find a baby lying in a manger, wrapped snugly in strips of cloth' (Lk 2:12). This message would convey a vital message to these men who were used to being scorned and abused for being 'unclean'. In their mind's eye, they would see a typical Palestinian one-room home with the familiar row of mangers strategically placed between the cattle's quarters and the family living area. They would also see a baby wrapped in strips of cloth – wrapped in the way their *own* babies were wrapped. In other words, they would realise that this baby had not been born into a palace from which they would be excluded. Rather, he was one of them. This was good news indeed! No wonder they *ran* from the fields into Bethlehem in search of the child!

By this time we were hooked by Ken Bailey's thesis. Now that our mind-set was more Middle Eastern than Western, it made perfect sense. But where did 'the inn' come in? The translators of the Gospel of Luke claim that Jesus was laid in a manger because 'there was no room for them in the inn' (Lk 2:7). We learned that day that the word Luke uses that has been translated 'inn' is *kataluma* (pronounced *kat-a-loom-a*). *'Kataluma'* simply means a place to stay. Luke uses this word on another occasion in his Gospel. On the night before he died, Jesus had a burning desire to share the Passover Feast with his disciples. When the disciples asked him where he wanted them to go to prepare for this meal, Jesus replied:

'As soon as you enter Jerusalem, a man carrying a pitcher of water will meet you. Follow him. At the house he enters, say to the owner, "The Teacher asks, Where is the *guest room* where I can eat the Passover meal with my disciples?" '

(Lk 22:10–11 NLT)

The Greek word that has been translated 'guest room' is *kataluma*. In other words, the *kataluma* is a large, furnished, upper room – the guest room; the kind of room the widow of Zarephath offered Elijah when he needed somewhere to stay.

While Luke uses the word *kataluma* for 'the guest room' he does not use this word when he re-tells Jesus' parable of the Good Samaritan who takes the man mugged on the road that runs between Jerusalem and Jericho to an inn. The word he uses for inn is *pandocheion* (pronounced *pan-dough-kee-on*) which means 'a public lodging place'.

Ken claimed, quietly, enthusiastically, persuasively, that what Luke is trying to convey is that Mary and Joseph travelled to Bethlehem because the census compelled Joseph to be there. They were provided with accommodation by relatives who gave them the privilege of sharing the family room with them. While they were there, Mary went into labour, Jesus was born and, in the absence of a crib, they laid him in a manger 'because there was no room for them in the guest room'. The guest room, doubtless, was being occupied by other relatives who were also visiting Bethlehem because of the census.

The atmosphere in the group was one of relief, joy and satisfaction. At last, here was an interpretation of the Gospel narrative that made sense in its cultural context. We hardly

needed Ken's final insights though we found them equally
persuasive. Reading again from Luke's Gospel, he reminded us
that, having visited the holy family, 'the shepherds returned
glorifying and praising God for all they had seen and heard' –
including the quality of the accommodation. We chuckled
when Ken asked, 'Would they have been glorifying and
praising God if they had found a baby lying in a dirty manger
in a draughty stable?' And we agreed with him when he
surmised that they would have insisted on transferring the
family from the stable to their own one-room home where they
could have been competently cared for.

The video ended, not with Ken's Bible open at Luke 2 but
at Matthew 2 where we read that, after the Magi had visited
Herod to ask where they might find the new-born King, the
star guided them to Bethlehem. 'It . . . stopped over the place
where the child was. When they saw the star, they were filled
with joy! They entered *the house* where the child and his
mother, Mary, were, and they fell down before him and worshipped him' (Mt 2:10,11 NLT emphasis mine). Matthew
makes no reference to an inn or a stable. He has the holy
family in a house.

The video ended. For several minutes no one spoke but
the atmosphere in the room was electric. Each of us had been
deeply touched by what we had seen and heard and felt.
Eventually, the young woman who had said to me earlier that
day, 'I just can't believe the Christmas story' broke the
silence. Everything had fallen into place for her. Now she was
ready to begin her retreat. Others then shared their response
to what we had seen and heard and felt. None of us had
remained unmoved or untouched. It was as though the
proverbial penny had dropped and we were poised to engage
with the Christmas story in an entirely new way. We had a
wonderful retreat!

Last Christmas, I showed the same video to a group of
people who had never been to the Middle East. Again, when

I switched the video off, there was silence – until one woman said, 'It all makes so much sense . . . I've always felt rather irritated with Joseph. He seemed so incompetent and irresponsible not making plans for Mary when he knew that the baby was due. Now I can warm to him because he comes across as caring and concerned – the kind of husband God *would* give to Mary.'

Notes

Introduction
1. Isaac Watts

Chapter 1
1. Carlo Carretto, *The God Who Comes* (London: DLT, 1977) p.xix
2. Source unknown.
3. David Adam, *Glimpses of Glory* (London: SPCK, 2000) p 5.
4. Joyce Huggett, adaptation of a prayer in *Approaching Christmas* (Oxford: Lion, 1987) p 9.

Chapter 2
1. Stephen Travis, *The Jesus Hope* (London: Word Books, 1974) p 92.
2. Metropolitan Anthony of Sourozh, *Living Prayer* (London: DLT, 1980) p 12.
3. Joyce Huggett, adaptation of a prayer in *Approaching Christmas* (Oxford: Lion, 1987) p 10.
4. William Young Fullerton.

Chapter 3
1. Adaptation of a prayer by Dean E. Milner White in *My God My Glory* (London: SPCK, Triangle, 1994) p 16. Reproduced by kind permission of the Friends of York Minster.

Chapter 4
1. An extract from *A Shalom Prayer* quoted with kind permission. The complete prayer is available on a leaflet from The Maranatha Community, 102, Irlam Road, Flixton, Manchester M41 6JT. This and other prayers are also available on the CD *Shalom* available from the same address.

Chapter 5
1. Marilyn Baker, *Changing Me.* (Eastbourne: Kingsway's Thank You Music, 1996). Used by permission of Thank You Music, PO Box 75, Eastbourne, East Sussex, BN23 6NW.

Chapter 6
1. Jim Packer, source not traced.
2. Edwin Hatch, 1835–1889.

Chapter 7
1. John Bunyan, *The Pilgrim's Progress* (London: Lutterworth Press, 1947) pp 160, 162.
2. Alcuin of York.

Chapter 8
1. Charles Wesley.
2. E.M. Blaiklock (Trans), *The Practice of the Presence of God* (London: Hodder & Stoughton, 1989) p 48.
3. David Adam, *The Cry of the Deer* (London: SPCK, Triangle, 1993) p 105.

4. Joyce Huggett, *Embracing God's World* (London: Hodder & Stoughton, 1996) p 177.
5. F. Dostoevsky, *The Brothers Karamazov*, quoted by Tony Castle, *A Treasury of Prayer* (London: Hodder & Stough-ton, 1993) p 82.
6. An adaptation of a Celtic prayer.

Chapter 9
1. Macrina Wiederkehr OSB, *A Tree Full of Angels: Seeing the Holy in the Ordinary* (San Francisco: HarperCollins, 1990) p 105.
2. Ibid. p 105.
3. Marilyn Baker, *The Father's Song of Love*. (Eastbourne: Kingsway's Thank You Music, 1996). Used by permission of Thank You Music, PO Box 75, Eastbourne, East Sussex, BN23 6NW.
4. Joyce Huggett, adaptation of a prayer in *Approaching Christmas* (Oxford: Lion, 1987) p 51.
5. David Adam, *Glimpses of Glory* (London: SPCK, 2000) p 41.

Chapter 10
1. Jean Vanier, *The Broken Body* (London: DLT, 1989) pp 73,74.
2. Ibid.
3. Janet Morley, *God With Us*, Christian Aid, 1989; quoted ed. Janet Morley, *Bread for Tomorrow* (London: SPCK, 1992) p 38.
4. From Scripture in Song, a division of Integrity Music. Copyright © 1977. Administered by Kingsway's Thank You Music, P O Box 75, Eastbourne, East Sussex BN23 6NW. For the territory of the UK only. Used by permission.
5. David Adam, *The Edge of Glory* (London: SPCK, 1985) p 34.

Chapter 11
1. Joseph Mohr translated by John Freeman Young.
2. Bill Volkman, *Basking in His Presence* (Illinois: Union Life, 1996) p 63.
3. Ibid. p 63.
4. Thomas Merton, found on a card. Source not traced.
5. Toki Miyashina, quoted in K.H. Strange and R.G.E. Sandback (compilers) *Psalm Twenty Three – An Anthology* (Scotland: St Andrew's Press, 1978).
6. David Adam, set to calming music by Margaret Rizza on the CD and cassette *Fire of Love*, published by Kevin Mayhew and on the *Joy to the World* CD
7. Source unknown.

Chapter 12
1. Ernest Boyer Jr, *Finding God at Home* (SanFrancisco: HarperCollins, 1988) p 56.
2. John Stott, *The Birds Our Teachers* (Candle Books: 1999) p 9.
3. Joni Eareckson Tada, *When Is It Right To Die? Suicide, Euthanasia, Suffering and Mercy* (Grand Rapids, MI: Zondervan, 1992) p 23–25; 178–9.

4. *The Iona Community Worship Book* (Glasgow: Wild Goose Publications, 1990, 1994). Text by John L. Bell and the Wild Goose Resource Group © 1986. WGRG, Iona Community, 840 Govan Road, Glasgow G51 3UU, Scotland.

Chapter 13
1. Ephraim the Syriac.
2. Joyce Huggett, *Embracing God's World: A Special Collection of New and Classic Prayers* (London: Hodder & Stoughton, 1996) p 130. This prayer was written in Cyprus when I lived there. For some reason, Father Christmas almost always seems to be holding a dove there.

Chapter 14
1. David Adam, *The Rhythm of Life: Celtic Daily Prayer* (London: SPCK, Triangle, 1996) pp 48–49.

Chapter 15
1. Sr Lisbeth CHN (transl) *Mary's Key: A Guided Walk With Mary Through Her Song of Praise* (Sweden: Stiftelsen Vete-komet, no date).
2. J.I. Packer, *Keep In Step With the Spirit* (Leicester: IVP, 1985) p 12.
3. J.I. Packer, *Laid Back Religion* (Leicester: IVP, 1989) p 100.
4. Marilyn Baker, *Rest in My Love*. Word's Spirit of Praise Music/Copycare.
5. *A Shalom Prayer*, The Maranatha Community, Manchester.

Chapter 16
1. Carmen L. Caltagirone, *Friendship as Sacrament* (Manila: St Paul Publications, 1989) p 5.
2. Ibid. p 7.
3. Ibid. p 28.
4. Ibid. p 15.

Chapter 17
1. Culled from an article by Dick Innes in *Psychology for Living*, Nov/Dec 2000. Published by The Narramore Christian Foundation.
2. Elizabeth Ruth Obbard, *Magnificat* (London: DLT, 1985) p 82.
3. Hymn For Vespers on the Feast of the Visitation of the Virgin Mary, *Office Book of the Community of the Holy Name,* Derby, 1988, p 308.

Chapter 18
1. *The Iona Community Worship Book* (Wild Goose Publications, 1990, 1994), p 49. Text by John L Bell and the Wild Goose Resource Group © 1986, WGRG, Iona Community, 840 Govan Road, Glasgow G51 3UV, Scotland.
2. William Barclay, Daily Study Bible: The Gospel of John, Volume 1 (Edinburgh: The St Andrew Press) adaptation of days 21,30.
3. John Wimber, arranged and sung by Jane Lilley on the *Joy to the World* CD and cassette.
4. Philip Yancey, *What's So Amazing About Grace?* (London: HarperCollins,

1997) p 70.
5. Jim Packer, *Laid-Back Religion,* (Leicester: IVP, 1989) p 101.
6. Janet Morley, All Desires Known, (London: SPCK).
7. Joyce Huggett, adaptation of a prayer in *Embracing God's World* (London: Hodder & Stoughton, 1996) p 131.

Chapter 19
1. Joseph's Song, Michael Card, © Sparrow Song/EMI Christian Publishing. Administered by Copycare, P O Box 77, Hailsham, BN2 7EF, UK/ Music@copycare.com. Used by permission.
2. David Adam, *The Rhythm of Life* (London: SPCK, 1996) p 122.

Chapter 20
1. Michael Riddell, *Godzone* (Oxford: Lion Publishing, 1992) p 37.
2. W. Morrice, 'Joy in the New Testament', *New Unger's Bible Dictionary* (Chicago: Moody Press, 1988) p 417.
3. Michael Riddell, op. cit. p 10.
4. Sr. Pamela Hayes © Kevin Mayhew Ltd.
5. Prayer of the Heart: part of the Cuthbert Liturgy *Into a Desert Place* from Celtic Daily Prayer by the Northumbria Community (London: HarperCollins, 2000) p 176.

Chapter 21
1. John Chrysostom, *Quod Christus sit Deus* No. 3.

Chapter 22
1. Walter Wangerin, *The Book of God* (Oxford: Lion Publishing, 1996) pp 597–598.
2. W. Muir, The Prayer of St Columba quoted in *Celtic Daily Prayer* (London: HarperCollins, 2000) p 352.

Chapter 23
1. David Adam, *The Edge of Glory* (London: SPCK, Triangle, 2000) p 11.
2. Peter Marshall, source not traced.

Chapter 24
1. Matthew Henry, *Commentary of the Whole Bible* (London: Marshall, Morgan and Scott, 1960) p 216.
2. Joyce Huggett, *Embracing God's World* (London: Hodder & Stoughton, 1996) p 142.

Chapter 25
1. Jocelyn G. Murray, *Windows on Widowhood* (Godalming: Highland Books, 1995) p 20.
2. Ibid. p 22.
3. Sue Monk Kidd, *When the Heart Waits* (San Francisco: Harper SanFrancisco, 1990) pp13,26.
4. Professor James Fowler quoted ibid. p 123.

5. Declaration of Faith from Morning Prayer in *Celtic Daily Prayers* by the Northumbria Community, (London: HarperCollins, 2000) p.17. Set to music that is available on the CD from The Northumbria Community – available on CD from The Northumbria Community Cloisters, Hetton Hall, Chatton, Northumberland NE66 5SD)
6. Joyce Huggett, adaptation of a prayer in *Embracing God's World* (London: Hodder & Stoughton, 1996) p 141.

Chapter 26
1. Thomas Merton. Source not found.
2. William Temple. Source not traced.
3. Adaptation of a Celtic prayer.
4. Joyce Huggett.
5. Declaration of Faith from Morning Prayer in *Celtic Daily Prayer* by the Northumbria Community, (London: HarperCollins, 2000) p 17.

Chapter 27
1. Taken from *The Singer* by Calvin Miller, © 1975, 2001, pp 102–103. Used by permission of InterVarsity Press, PO Box 1400, Downers Grove, IL 60515.
2. From a Christmas card produced by the Sisters of the Community of the Holy Name, Derby.
3. From a new unfolding of Psalm 51 by Jim Cotter, *Healing – more or less* (Sheffield: Cairns Publications, 1990) pp 58,59.
4. Isaiah 9:2 The Message, The Old Testament Prophets in contemporary language.
5. Isaiah 60:19 The Message, The Old Testament Prophets in contemporary language.
6. Psalm 36:9 The Message (Psalms).
7. John 1:5 The Message.

Chapter 28
1. My adaptation of a Celtic prayer.
2. Joyce Huggett, *Embracing God's World* (London: Hodder & Stoughton, 1996) p 172.

Chapter 29
1. Joyce Huggett, ibid, p 141.
2. Eddie Askew, *A Silence and a Shouting* (Brentford: The Leprosy Mission, 1993) p 45.
3. African Prayer for Refugees quoted *The Iona Community Worship Book* (Wild Goose Publications, 1991) p 59.

Chapter 30
1. Alfred Edersheim, *The Life and Times of Jesus the Messiah* (London: Longmans, Green and Co, 1906) p 214.
2. Christina Georgina Rossetti 1830–94.

3. Adaptation of a song composed by Barry McGuire and Mike Deasy, arranged by David Peacock, copyright Sparrow song/Cherry Lane Music Ltd. Sung by the Jane Lilley Singers on the CD and cassette *The Saviour's Day* (Guildford: Eagle Publishing) and *Joy to the World*.
4. Janet Morley, *All Desires Known* (London: SPCK, 1992) p 7.

Chapter 31
1. Sue Ashdown, quoted in Joyce Huggett, *Embracing God's World* (London: Hodder & Stoughton, 1996) pp 94–95.

Chapter 32
1. Richard Foster's often quoted phrase.
2. Peter Dodson, *Contemplating the Word* (London: SPCK, 1987) p 1.
3. Ernest Boyer, Jr, *Finding God in the Home* (San Francisco: Harper SanFrancisco, 1988) pp 17,19.
4. Ibid. p 94.
5. Ibid. p 58.
6. Ibid. p 95.

Chapter 33
1. Minnie Louse Haskins. Found on a prayer card. Quoted by King George VI in a Christmas broadcast, 1939.
2. Charlotte Elliott 1789–1871.
3. Helen Mallicout. Found on a poster. Source not traced.

Chapter 34
1. Paul Flucke, *The Secret of the Gifts* (Illinois: InterVarsity Press, 1992) p 10.
2. Ibid. p 11.
3. Ibid. p 14.
4. Ibid. p 20.
5. Ibid. p 22.
6. St Clare. Found on a prayer card produced by the Community of St Clare, Freeland, Oxford.

Picture Credits

All pictures are used with the kind permission of the artists.

Sister Theresa Margaret CHN © pp. 18, 43, 59, 76, 80, 117, 124, 129, 141, 143, 174, 179, 189, 192.

Sister Irene CHN © p. 94.

Sister Elizabeth Obbard © pp. 38, 108.

Sister Gael O'Leary RSM © p. 102.

The Rev. David Chance © p. 16.

Joan Hutson © pp. 23, 34, 70, 81, 161, 168.

David G. Klein © p. 88.

Nancy Ruth Jackson © p. 49.

Joyce Cheverton © pp. 31, 111, 135, 150, 157, 201, 206.

Open to God

JOYCE HUGGETT

Over 40,000 copies sold

In Open to God Joyce Huggett addresses some of the 'barriers and blocks' to a deeper prayer life, offering practical guidance on how to prepare for prayer and find stillness. How to use the body and the imagination and how to enjoy whole days of prayer and meditation.

Open to God also includes twenty-eight meditations, using biblical readings and other material as a springboard for a closer encounter with God. The theme of new beginnings makes them ideal for use at any time the reader is called to a deeper and richer prayer life.

* * *

To accompany this book, Eagle have also produced a cassette tape containing meditative instrumental music and heart-stirring songs which can be used either alongside the meditations presented in *Open to God*, or simply played on its own for pure pleasure.

0 86347 229 X (book)
0 86347 241 9 (tape)

Hearing Jesus
Jesus' teaching in its cultural context
JOYCE HUGGETT – 0 86347 304 0

Patterns in Prayer (tape)
Prayers and meditations with music
ANGELA ASHWIN – 0 86347 093 9

Patterns Not Padlocks
For parents and all busy people
ANGELA ASHWIN – 0 86347 088 2

Personality and Prayer
Prayer to match your personality
DR RUTH FOWKE – 0 86347 209 5

Praying Our Goodbyes
Examining the spirituality of change
JOYCE RUPP – 0 86347 154 4

The Sounds of God
Hearing the voice of God
MICHAEL MITTON – 0 86347 067 X

Spiritual Friendship
A guide for prayer companions
WENDY MILLER – 0 86347 129 3

Conflict

JOYCE HUGGETT

Understanding, managing and growing through conflict.

Unresolved conflict destroys marriages and friendships,
families and fellowships, businesses and churches – even
missionary organisations. Yet Christians are rarely equipped
with the tools needed to handle contaminated relationships.

Conflict, by Joyce Huggett, seeks to provide such tools. It
begins with the good news that conflict has a positive face.
The author exposes the ways in which Jesus himself grew
through clashes of various kinds and examines reasons why
friction frequently disrupts relationships. *Conflict* claims
that handled creatively, quarrels and collisions can
become the nerve-centre of growth.

Because conflict is an inevitable fact of life, each chapter ends
with exercises aimed to enable the readersto process friction in
such a way that it results in the up-building, rather than the
downfall of relationships.

0 86347 075 0